ROCK ON BY

RACHEAL CARDISS

Ordering Information:

Prime Seven Media
518 Landmann St.
Tomah City, WI 54660

Printed in the United States of America

DEDICATION

This book is dedicated to my mother [deceased] and grandfather [deceased] for their positive attitudes have always been a part of who I am. My husband, our children. Thank you all for your support and always believing in me. Last but not least my family and friends for your encouragement and positivity.

CONTENTS

FOREWARD

From a very young age, Craig's son Jamie. Has been fascinated, regularly watching the trains. Once a week the shiny, elegant express train travels past. Jamie, imagines. The passengers lives. All from the comfort of his veranda. He wonders, 'where they may be headed? Where they'd come from? Would they have a great love story to share? Or worse a tragic tale to tell? Jamie felt there was something soothing about the familiarity those trains bring as they rock on by. When he wasn't riding or watching trains. You'd find him building model railroads. Jamie always did well at geography and debate his mother often said to Craig our boy will be a travelling lawyer. Nah, he likes building with Lego and blocks. My guess, a conductor or an engineer.

His daughter Lucy didn't share her brother's love of trains. Her passion is horses. At school, Lucy excelled at agricultural studies and home economics. It is her dream, to one day work on a horse ranch. 'Shearer' is the name of Lucy's horse. She was given him for her 4th birthday, you could say they've grown up together. He has white boots a light brown, caramel coloured coat. With various white patches. Full brown mane and tail.

My Family Tree

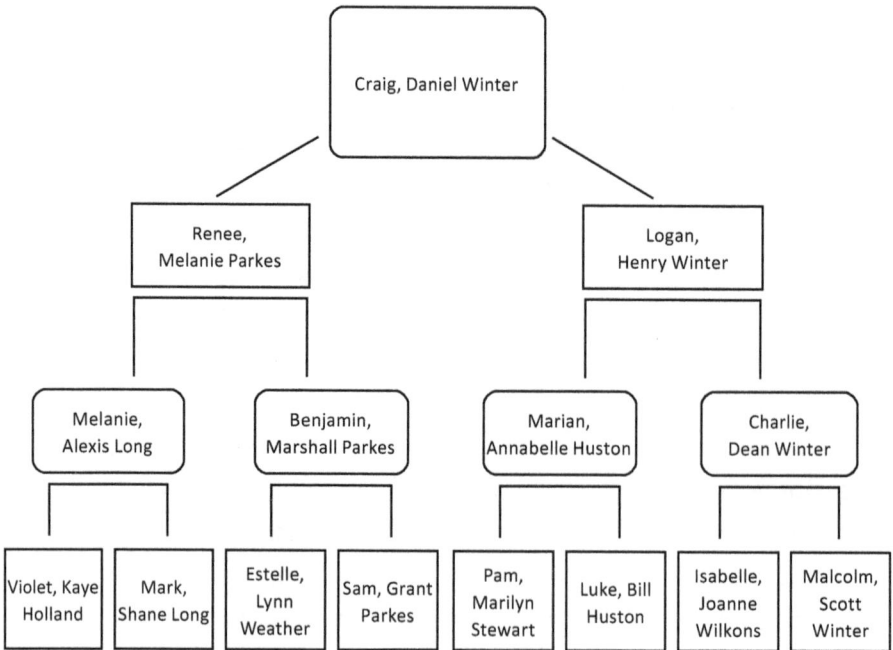

Craig, Daniel Winter

- **Renee, Melanie Parkes**
  - **Melanie, Alexis Long**
    - Violet, Kaye Holland
    - Mark, Shane Long
  - **Benjamin, Marshall Parkes**
    - Estelle, Lynn Weather
    - Sam, Grant Parkes
- **Logan, Henry Winter**
  - **Marian, Annabelle Huston**
    - Pam, Marilyn Stewart
    - Luke, Bill Huston
  - **Charlie, Dean Winter**
    - Isabelle, Joanne Wilkons
    - Malcolm, Scott Winter

Chapter One

06th of March 1991, 'Winter Forth.'

Turning onto his street, Craig felt a comfortable, familiar feeling. He was almost home, they're here. Craig stepped down, off the school bus at the top of his driveway. He then began aimlessly wandering around. If anyone happened to pass by or was sitting on their front veranda watching him. They could have easily felt, how uncontrollably upset and frustrated he was by an inadequate mobile service. "Damn!," he exclaimed. I can't read Russell's message. Usually we ride the bus home together, but not today. Directly after school he went away with he's family. And isn't expected to return until Sunday afternoon. (ding!) Message; 'service unavailable.' Craig believes, it is due to a long row of trees along the side of the road. He said to himself "Why these were so essential?, I'll never understand!" But to quote farmer Garth [our right side neighbour] 'They provide privacy!' "Argh! Still nothing." I'll just check it again when I get inside the house. Craig continued walking down his driveway. Which was only 300m long. He saw their two storey manor. Family dog Angus, on the veranda patiently awaiting Craig's arrival. Just out front from the veranda steps is a small round turning circle, which also features a garden. When dad cleared the dirt to form the driveway, he built it up and the soil is at the gardens base. To the left of the turning circle is the double garage, to the right is a Beautiful outdoor sitting area. Earlier today I received a message from Russell, that read. "Hey, mate. Chloe, wishes to meet up with you at the library next week. I'll text you her phone number before I leave this afternoon. Russell" I've yet to mention my interest in Chloe to my mum. She has some idea of me dating the daughter of one of her RWA (Rural Women's Association) friends. Penelope, somebody? Anyway, Penelope Biggs. That's it Biggs. Turned up here, a few weeks ago with her daughter Charlotte. Because as my mum put it. "thought you two can be friends." If mum happens to bring up the issue again. I'll tell her about Chloe then. Naturally in a matter of fact kind of way. Beginning with, "A girl agreed to give me her phone number today!" Ugh! frustration, [looking at phone] still not available! At school, many women have admired Craig's deep, adorable brown eyes, shoulder length brown curly hair. But Chloe, is the only girl he has fancied, ever since her family moved here last month. Craig recalls the time clearly because he'd just turned 16, three days earlier. Craig is fairly confidant in approaching people by himself. But since she and his best friend Russell, share five lessons a day together. Russell assured him by saying, "I'll speak to her, during history today." Craig has lived here at 'Winter Forth' his whole life. The farm is located 100kms north of the town, Hillstem in QLD. 'Winter Forth' has been in Craig's family for four generations. After showering and sitting down in the lounge room. Craig retrieved his mobile from his school bag. Now I'm connected to the home internet. Crossing my fingers, I'm hoping to see a new message from Russell. [ding, ding!] Oh! Yes, here it is, thanks Rus. Bugger! To my dismay, it's just a notification. Informing me of service availability. It had become, evident from an early age that Craig Winter, had quite the talent for woodworking. His father Logan is a skilled carpenter. So it was no surprise to anyone that 'building' and 'designing' were two of Craig's favourite subjects in school. Craig, applies many of the skills he'd learnt from he's father, grandfather and great, great grandfather, Malcolm Winter. A contract builder, who worked for the local council during his years here at 'Winter Forth.' With so much knowledge and experience for him to look up to. It's no wonder that Craig has talent, and ambition.

Chapter Two

Craig's project

For as long as Craig can recall, he dreams of one day becoming a carpenter, just like his father Logan. Craig, began as many people usually do. Designing a project that's close to home. This proved to be a very realistic possibility. All the wood he could need. Could be sourced from the farm. Outside one beautiful afternoon in September. Craig found himself, walking along the driveway. He then stood still staring. Suddenly his gaze met the line of oak trees along the left hand side. There are oak trees along both sides. But for some reason the ones on the left, fascinated Craig more. He mentally admired their height, bases, and natural carvings as well as their outstretched branches. [brilliant idea] Craig said to himself. Hmm, if I…. yes? Then I could….., I'm certain, if I ask dad. He'll put one trunk in the garage for me. Craig excitedly stated aloud. "This will be great!" those trees, they look similar to those darn trees which interfere with internet signal. Dad and his business partner usually prune them around spring. They lop down older ones and plant saplings in their place. It isn't a worldly recognized holiday. But certainly a tradition celebrated around here. Everyone marks birthdays, anniversaries, appointments off their calendars. My family, countdown the days until 'Spring Sapling Saturday' this is what my dad Logan calls it. He then went looking for his dad. Logan agreed. Replying "me and Frank

Murphy will be cutting this lot on the coming weekend mate! The trunk will be in there for you by Monday afternoon. What are you planning to do my boy?," enquired Logan. Craig replied "You'll see" He was so excited! He could hardly wait. (Monday afternoon) Craig entered the garage and there upon the bench he saw the smooth, debarked trunk. He looked it over, while running his fingers along the length of it. Thinking this will be plenty big enough. He walked back into the kitchen. To thank his father, Logan. Who was just thanking he's mate, Frank Murphy. Frank came around as promised to help cut down the trees and clean them.

- "Oh Craig, you remember. Mr Murphy from down the road? He helped me with the trunk and carrying it in there for you."
- "I do, thanks Dad and thankyou Mr Murphy. I can't wait to get started."

Craig spent the rest of the afternoon in the garage. He tidied up, moved things around, swept. Whilst clearing benches, he did a general inventory of his dad's tool collection and re arranged them. Craig's mother Renee, knew how passionate. Craig was when he set his mind to something. 'Winter Forth' was not only a large estate, it's also a working farm. Hence, there is always something that needs tending to. His mother Renee, understood that Craig's chores would no doubt suffer as a result to his dedication. 3.30pm Renee, heard the school bus pull up. Any moment now Craig would pedal up to the house on his push bike. Shadowed closely by his younger brother Wilson. Wilson was around the same height as Craig though he was 4 years younger.

He doesn't sport the curly hair like Craig or grandma Marian. He prefers it kept short like his dad Logan. Wilson got off of his bike, placed his bag just inside the door then casually headed upstairs to his room. Craig's feet barely touched the ground before he tossed his bag onto the veranda. No one is certain, how he managed it? But after being in his room for under 3 mins. Craig emerged, fully changed. Then he darted out to the garage. Each afternoon this became routine. Even on some weekends, soon after breakfast. Whoosh! He's gone. Craig, was rarely seen. He did however get seen waltzing in and through the kitchen. Then tangoing back out again. A 1litre juice in his left hand and a stack of sandwiches in his right. Once inside the garage, he shut the doors behind him. Then was scarcely seen until dinner. When anyone happened to run into Craig along the veranda or in the kitchen. They tried enquiring? Asking Craig, "how is your.......? Or how much longer? Will it be a.....?" all enquiries were met with a quick "you'll see!" Then off he went again. His project took Craig a little under two months. Sitting out the front one afternoon. Logan and Renee said to each other.

-   "You know, if it weren't for the noise and the empty food trays. One could forget Craig was even home! I'll bet it's a secret gift, for someone special at school. Like a jewellery or pencil box?"
-   "To my knowledge, no one has gotten an explanation, a hint or answers as yet!"
-   Logan, then said. "Speculation is really all, any of us have to go on."

[Reveal] The morning has finally arrived. Craig happily enters the kitchen and announces. "Come on, everyone join me on the front veranda please?" When his mother got out there. she immediately began glancing around the veranda. Having a thorough look, she got a puzzled look on her face. Everything appeared where it should be. So, she said to herself. What could that lad need us all out here for? One last look. But, Wait! She saw the corner of the veranda. There is a noticeable difference. It looks as though something is leaning up against the bannister, next to the arch. Hmm? Only it appears covered over with...?

- "HEY!, CRAIG DANIEL WINTER, I'VE BEEN LOOKING FOR THAT SHEET!" said his mother crossly.
- Craig looked around, then asked "Is everyone here? [roll call] "Wilson, mum, dad, Mrs Sherwood, grandad Charlie and Gra...... Hold on! Where is grandma?"
- "Over here my boy" [coming out of the kitchen] answers grandma Marian.

She goes to take a seat, by the stairs. Craig, suddenly and loudly cries out "WAIT! [Calmer], Gran sit here." He lifted up the sheet to reveal a beautifully designed wooden rocking chair. Craig gave his grandma a big hug. Then she sat down. He then walked over to his mother.

- "I'm sorry about the sheet mum, I should have asked you. I'm happy to give it a wash."
- "That's ok boy, the chair looks really good. So this is what you've been up to! Great job dear."
- "It really is remarkable, a great design and quality. And your grandma appears comfortable, leaning back and all." added he's father Logan.

Heading to university March 1993.

Craig is now 18. And soon he will be moving to Ashhern, [4 hours away] with three close friends. Russell, Kenneth and William, where they'll attend university together. Craig, always looked up to his father. For as long as he can remember, his only wish is to become a fully qualified carpenter. Then Craig can professionally and confidently work alongside him. Russell, who has been Craig's best friend since kindergarten. Lives two driveways down from 'Winter Forth' to the left. Craig met the other two lads in high school, around year 8. Kenneth and William, were both born in and live in Sagehurst. [30 mins from Hillstem]. The first semester break, won't be until six months after enrolment. Kenneth's uncle Morgan, owns a 3 bedroom house in Ashhern. With a 32 foot granny flat at the rear. Everyone will live there with him. From there it's a short bus ride to the university. Craig will share some classes with Kenneth and William. But many of the same classes with Russell. Who is a fellow gifted designer, also planning on becoming a carpenter. Kenneth, is studying to be a lawyer. Kenneth is of medium height, I guess cuddly. Would be an accurate, polite term. He has short red hair, blue eyes, a moustache and a long beard, same colour as his hair. Which according to him he 'trained' to grow down from his sideburns. To look at him you can't tell where the moustache finishes and the beard begins? Intrigued, people have often asked him, how? They have even tried to touch it. Kenneth simply moves their hand away from his face and says. "Ah, ah. I trained it well!" he then runs his fingers through his beard. It is said that most people wish to forget high school nicknames. But Kenneth often called [Gnome] remembers he's fondly. In fact many of his friends still call him this today. University will be for 3-4 years. Upon hearing this news, Kenneth was utterly disappointed that he's unable to bring along his Harley Davidson motorcycle for the duration. Lovingly referred to as 'Harliqueen.' She will instead be safely parked up in his parents garage. William, believe it or not is lovingly nicknamed 'Wilma.' Yes, lovingly! I don't understand how a nickname is something to be proud of? If you think about it. "Michelle is Shelly, Edward can be Edward Eddie, Ed or playfully Edwardo. Jamie or Jason is Jay. Those names can at least be worn with pride, even accidently. But to so proudly stand by Gnome and Wilma, hmm? It just does my head in at times. Since age 5, Wilma had been teased. He was tall, wore glasses and had long, thin black hair. I wouldn't say scrawny.

Athletic, I suppose. The bullying experience made him shy and withdrawn. Some even started saying he appeared 'girly' hence the Wilma. I remember when Wilma developed his first crush. He became really sensitive. Still remained withdrawn. We often found him starring up into the clouds.

Everyone knew he liked this girl, Natalie.....? Can't remember her last name! After two to three awkward weeks of blushing whenever he saw her. Ducking in behind library shelves. Doing tuckshop dashes. [He collected ordered lunch, then dashed off again.] Eating lunch on the oval, so as to avoid seeing her in the undercover area.

To this day, we still don't know exactly what? Or how it happen? It was after school finished, the buses arrived. Wilma emerged, hair neatly tied back, shirt tucked in even shoelaces tied. He walked straight toward Natalie. And asked her to meet him at the local café, later this afternoon. We could hardly believe it. And we just saw it! Wilma had finally crept out of his shell. First few times, Natalie replied no. We were all convinced he'd recede back into the comfort of his shell. But Wilma surprised us all. He kept persisting. He was so pleased when Natalie......? Darn, I always forget her last name. I know, I know it but oh! Ah! It'll come to me later. Anyway she'd finally agreed to go out with him. Craig, suddenly shouted out 'got it! I knew, I knew it! Withers. That's her last name!' Kenneth [Gnome] wasn't the only one of us who would miss 'Harliqueen.' Craig got to ride her a couple of times when they visited the beginners track at 'Rear Tyre.' 'Rear tyre' is a local track not far from the town of Hillstem. It features many large open areas. Designated to bike riders, both bicycle and motorbikes as well as drivers wanting to playfully race and egg each other on with questions like. "Are we ever going to have a chicken race?" Equestrian riders were also welcome. There's an obstacle course with different difficulty levels, depending on chosen track size; Small, medium, or large. All courses contain jumps and tight corners. This is where the three of them were usually found of a Saturday afternoon. Gnome was the only one of their group who could legally drive, passing his provisional driving test just last month. Craig and William, grew up on farms. Often driving tractors and quad bikes around their grounds. They each had driving lessons with their dad's. But as yet no on road driving experience. 'Rear Tyre' has a 6X6 stable, coincidentally designed and built by Craig's father Logan and some of his co-workers. The stable stands alongside a 100 metre track. Visitors are encouraged to bring their own horse. However, there's usually 3-5 horses if you'd like to hire them. Wilma, didn't share this leisure time with them. He usually sat up in the grand stands alone and played games on his mobile. We often saw or heard his frustrations, cursing over some aspect of the game he was playing. Gnome and Craig, often teased him by saying.

- "You working out our finances up there mate? Is that what's got you so upset? Something just not adding up?"
- "Let me guess, we can't actually afford to keep coming here?" Gnome added.
- They both laugh. "Come on mate, join us."
- Wilma quickly retorted with a "Oh, knock it off fellas! You know I'm messaging with my friend, Amoli Khatri from Delhi, India. Our eight month online chess game, is slowly reaching its conclusion. With each move getting more and more intense than the last. When he fi......."

[mobile dings] "darn! That was a real good move Amoli." [he thought to himself] Wilma has always been the smartest one amongst them. So it was no surprise when he announced 'I'm going to be an accountant!'

Chapter Three

❦

September 10ᵗʰ 1993, Semester one break

Gnome pulled up out the front of Ashhern University. Wilma and Craig were waiting for him on a bench by the entrance. Russell walked over to the car from reception. He tossed his bags into the boot and took the seat in behind Gnome. Wilma took the passenger side next to Gnome. Just as Craig hopped in the back behind Wilma.

- He asked "Russell, that graphics test we had yesterday bro? Did you find it as challenging as I did? Or did you not worry about it?"
- Russell replied. "No, I wasn't worried. I do however feel that I messed up the visual part of the exam. Why I thought my cabinet needed a detailed schematic of how my pin code lock would work, I'll never know?"
- Wilma then said "I found some of the research material was hard but mostly I enjoyed the challenge. Natalie and I have been a part of this awesome study group."
- Russell, Craig and Gnome all said in unison "study group?"
- "Yeah! They meet each Tuesday and Thursday night up in the campus library for an hour and a half. It's really been of

great help. All the material gets broken down into smaller manageable tasks."

Gnome will be dropping Craig and Russell at the bus station in town. Then he and Wilma will head on to the airport. Gnome is spending his 3 week break with 'Harliqueen.' Oh, ah. Excuse me. His mum in NSW [laughs] I'll bet whilst he is there, he'll ride his Harley. Wilma is flying to South Australia. He's agreed to help his sister Judith. He'll be housesitting, taking care of his nephew, and looking after her dog. [4 hours later] Renee and Logan met Craig and Russell at the bus terminal, in Hillstem. Craig knew he was almost home, the minute his dad turned into their street. When they got further along, Craig began to smile, admiring the familiar sight and sounds of the railroad on the opposite side of the road. Russell got dropped off at his place. [left of 'Winter Forth.'] They then continued into their own driveway. Passing the wooden mailbox, lovingly crafted by his father. Though, Craig just has to add "I made the chimney!" The aroma of the freshly harvested wheat fields. The line of oak trees running along both sides of their driveway. Soon after getting out of the car, Craig got bombarded with tail wags and licks from their dog Angus. Craig grabbed his bag and stepped inside. The first person he saw was their housekeeper/cook Mrs Sherwood. She tried to throw her arms around him and embrace him. Yet being a short woman, this always proved difficult for her. Craig, being the gentlemen he is, bent down to her. She then kissed him on his cheek and said happily "it is so good to see you!" Craig stood back up, closed his eyes and sniffed in deeply.

- [Moaning, mmm] "Is that an apple pie I smell?"
- "Yep! Just the way your grandma Marian makes it. Here lad, hand me that bag and I'll take it to your room. No doubt you've had some sort of dinner on your way home! I'll serve out the pie when I return."

- Just as Mrs. Sherwood turned around to leave. Craig asked "uh, Meredith…. You said, just like grandma Marian makes?" he rubbed his hands together, licked his lips. "Does this mean there's fresh whipped cream and home-made custard too?"
- She looked back at him, smiled and replied "oh my, boy of course!"

Russell's house really isn't far away from here. Oh, darn it! Craig, now found himself wondering. "If he should have invited Russell home with him for a bit?" Craig didn't know then, but Russell will be sorry to learn there was an apple pie with fresh cream and custard. Craig decided "Nah! I won't rub it in." He then thought, I remember Mrs Thompson fondly. She's well known for her baking. Russell always bought the best homemade treats to school with him. In fact, I'll bet there's fresh blueberry muffins or pumpkin scones awaiting him in his kitchen! Though he's only home for three weeks. Craig is pleased to be back at 'Winter Forth.' He's missed seeing the small brook out back by the wheat field. When standing on the back veranda or looking out his bedroom window. Craig can admire the windmill. He missed 'Stallion' his father's horse. Then Craig suddenly got the idea of taking a ride on him along the billabong. But as it's getting dark. He'll go for a ride tomorrow, maybe Wilson would like to join him? Normally Craig rides around on his own horse 'Chester' but 3 days before we left Ashhern. Logan informed him that for the next two months. 'Chester' will be staying at Mr McCarthy's Ranch [next door] for studding. Which incidentally is where 'Chester' came from originally. Mr McCarthy lives about 300metres down the road from 'Winter Forth Farm' Russell is the next driveway after Mr McCarthy's. The next day, after his ride, Craig returned 'stallion' to the barn and gave him some feed. Then headed back inside to wash his hands. Along the way he'd passed the rocking chair he made for grandmother Marian when he was

16. [he thought] What a nice time that was and she absolutely loved it. According to mum whenever she comes over she still uses it. Craig made himself a cup of coffee, walked back out onto the veranda and sat down in the rocking chair. He sipped his coffee then placed it down on the table beside him. His mind begun thinking back over those long afternoons. He saw beyond the arch way, beyond the steps, beyond the garden/turning circle. He was now once again mentally staring at the oak trees along the driveway. As clear as the day he began his project. He seen the designing, the plaining, and the debarking process. And once again Craig felt all the excitement, anticipation that went into creating this chair. Truly he felt as if he were 16 again. As pleasant as those memories were. One unpleasant one, popped up. Presenting louder than the happy ones. Craig recalled the amount of times. When he said to his friends "I'm sorry", or "perhaps another time", "sorry, but I'd better get going." Friends, who wished he'd join them at the shop, grab lunch together, or maybe go see a movie.

Craig begun gently rocking back and forth. "They didn't understand," he ran his hands along the arm rests, sighed. Then quietly said. "I was working on something special." Craig knew he can't get that time back. But he can choose how to spend his time after finishing university. Until this very moment, Craig hadn't dwelled on what he may have missed out on back then. Craig took another sip of his coffee then started to ponder.

"What if I had gone on those lunch dates?, accepted an invite to the movies?, been involved in study dates? Where might I be now? or indeed, who might I be with now?" Nearly finishing his cuppa. An inevitable question crept into his mind, followed by an uneasy feeling. What is that? What is this feeling? That uncontrollable thought? Craig answered himself. "I know... It's that feeling as if something or someone is missing from my life." I've read about these kinds of feelings in books. I've had female friends yet I still always found myself dreaming of someone else. But who? She must be out there somewhere! I've just not met her yet.' After witnessing how Wilma braved rejection and humiliation to persistently pursue Natalie. I was renewed with hope. I called my grandfather Charlie and asked him.

- "Grandpa, how were you so sure grandma was the woman for you?" My grandfather Charlie, told me what his father, Malcolm had once told him.
- "My son, one day you'll meet a woman who when you see her. You'll instantly know/feel that this is the only woman your meant to have eyes for, for the rest of your life!" he paused... [I'm certain he looked over at my grandma and smiled]. Then he concluded "Once you find her, don't let her get away!"
- "Is that Craig? asked Marian. "I'd like to speak with him."
- Granddad Charlie then said. "Here my boy, your grandma would like to speak with you. I'll get back to work and let her hang up, alright? Love you my dear boy."
- "I love you too, grandpa. Bye."
- Grandma Marian said. "Craig, if I may. Allow me to share some of my own 'words of wisdom' are you ready dear? Trust that she'll come around. As soon as you look up from the ground!"
- Craig, puzzled said. "what!? Grandma, what does any of this have to do with the ground?"
- "It simply means, to begin looking for love. You must first stop looking for love."
- Still confused. Craig decided to swallow these pearls gracefully and said. "Thanks for the advice grandma. I love you, enjoy the rest of your afternoon."

Chapter Four

7th of January 1996, looking for love, or not

Craig has now graduated from university, a fully qualified carpenter. Many people who achieve this need to then begin working or honing their trade. I've been assisting my dad and grandpa. Ever since I first held a hammer and could carry wood. Dad assures me there isn't work he needs assistance with at 'Winter Forth.' At the moment. Craig, sat down in the outdoor sitting area, opposite the turning circle. Started thinking, what are other ways I can keep myself busy? I know, I'll experiment with new designs and materials? I can do wood carving? Some of his mates believed they'd help him pass the time, by arranging blind dates. Craig accepted them though not gracefully, due to having prior reservations. They all started out nice and it seemed like they'd shared similar interests but he still hadn't yet felt that wow! This is her feeling, that Grandpa told him about. The advice his grandparents gave him nearly 3 years ago. Had puzzled Craig at the time. Lately though it has been playing over and over in his mind. Craig decided, I must go speak with grandma and granddad personally. So he drove into Hillstem. [knock! Knock.]

- A reply answered, "come in! Ah Craig, my boy. What can we help you with? Are you home? or on another break?" Asked Marian.

Craig sat down on the three seater couch, beside his grandma Marian. The couch was one of seven pieces. Beautifully nestled in the lounge room corner of their three bedroom home. Craig remembered when he was younger. He ran in, kicked his shoes against the wall and jumped onto the end piece. Then stretched out fully. It felt like he was in a single bed.

- "I'm home." He then cleared his throat and continued grandma. "I've come to ask you about something that's been puzzling me. Just how am I meant to find true love, if I'm not looking?'
- Marian, put aside her book. Turned to Craig and replied "it's the law of attraction my dear!" Craig, sat there silently. Possibly more confused than their last conversation.

Marian continued. "Let me tell you a story. A very similar thing happened here, just last month with your grandad. It was a Tuesday afternoon. Miserable rainy, windy weather. Everywhere outside was cold and wet. Grandpa Charlie couldn't do any work in the yard. Did he read? No. Did he watch TV? No. Was he prompted to start looking around inside [rolls her eyes] checking door knobs, tap handles, cupboards, and windows. Yes! My goodness, if it had a wobble, it rolled or shook and don't even get me started on creaking or squeaking. Then it got marked for fixing. The noise, not just from the power tools. Banging and hammering also.

"To this day Im unsure as to how he actually got any work completed? Because from our bedroom It sounded like more tools had been dropped than actually got used. Also, I wasn't there beside him, and to my knowledge no one dropped by. The volume of the cursing I heard. I was convinced, he was talking to someone. Things like; blast it! Where is my....? Aww! Mother #@%*..! No! I need the long handled... darn thingy.... Before I do that job! Then a nope, can't complete this either without my..... Then in he strolled into our room. Tipping over and removing drawers from our bedside tables and our dresser. The top shelf in our wardrobe always wobbled. One of the drawers from the dresser got stuck, when retracting back into place.

"I was sitting in the corner of our room, reading quietly well "trying" to. Frustrated by his discovery he walked out. And within a few minutes. [silence] Pure bliss. I'd heard nothing! I remember, because I thought he's having a nap on the lounge, ah! 'peace and quiet.' Now I can return to my book. Then he suddenly called out to me from the hallway."

- "Honey, where is my? SaaaAAW? Voice soft at first then got louder as he approached. He's now standing in our bedroom doorway. He continued, "my saw, I thought I'd left it under the laundry sink! But no!"
- I then asked him, "what have you lost dear? You can't find what?"
- "My saw!"
- I told him "never mind dear, I'm sure it will turn up. Try doing something else for a while and come back to it later."
- "Perhaps you're right." He said.

Then your grandad Charlie walked away. I heard the jug, so he must be making a coffee. No more than 2-3minutes had passed and I heard a loud 'I GOT IT!' Charlie appeared in our doorway again. I thought, 'how thoughtful he's bringing me in a coffee'.. but no.

- Charlie, stood in the doorway. Slightly out of breath and repeated "I got it!"

- I put my book down, again. And confusingly said "what? Wait! Hang on, I just said to go do something else. Why were you still looking?"
- Charlie replied, "I know, that's what you said, hon." I did do something else. I turned the kettle on intending to make a pot of coffee. Then I said. "Actually, I feel like tea." I opened the cupboard, reached in for the tea pot and saw this [holding up a stanley knife] "then the saws location came to me."
- "Great dear, so you'll continue with the drawers?"
- "No!" he said harshly.
- "No? Ok now, I'm confused. You're telling me I'm gonna have to trip over these damn drawers tonight on my way to bed!?" Marian replied crossly.
- "I can't repair them! It's not here!" A frustrated Charlie answered. He then continued, you see. "I lent it to our neighbour Ernie. And he let me borrow his stanley knife. To cut the Lino, for our laundry floor. I just wanted to come and thank you for your help, my dear."
- Now even more confused. Marian stated "What! Are you talking about Charlie?, I didn't realise it!"
- "No, but once, I'd stopped looking it for it. It came to me, just like you said it would."
- "Oh, ah, you're welcome I guess"
- "There you have it Craig, an example of how 'The law of attraction' works. 7 out of 10 times, it's effective. The other 3, [shrugs her shoulders] We obviously can't count on. Or we would have won the lottery by now!"
- "Thank you grandmother for sharing this story with me."
- "That's ok dear, can I get you something? We have biscuits, a shepherd's pie, left over pizza. Have you eaten?"
- "No, I'm all good gran, Mrs Sherwood is doing her famous roast beef tonight and you know how filling that can be!" in

fact, I'd better get going. Hugs his grandma and granddad and heads towards the door.

- Ok bye, Marian calls out "Please send my love to your mum, dad and Wilson." She then resumes her book.

[after dinner] Logan, came and sat down next to Craig at the dinner table. Turned to Craig and said "son, you know I've been making those regular trips to pick up timber, visit with suppliers and or contractors?"

- "Yeah, wow! They've been every few months for around four years now."
- "That's right, boy. Well I was just thinking about some of the trips I made with Robert Evans. You know he was welcomed company for me during your time at university --."
- Craig [interrupted] "do you mean the Robert, who moved into the house on our right with his family when he was only five."
- "That's him."
- "Wow! He's gotta be at least 22 now, right?"
- "Yeah, about that. We met him during that five month period where we were living in the town of Hillstem. Do you remember that? Your mother needed to be close. She was caring for her father, your grandad Benji."
- Craig began to wonder. Then asked, "where is Robert nowadays dad?, The last time I saw him, he and Vanessa had just welcomed their son Troy."
- 'Yep, then they all moved in with Vanessa's family. "Troy, was born partially deaf. They'll be a lot closer to that special school Troy will later need to attend. Logan continued, 'Robert's Parents, retired to Tempurst, NSW. There they bought a two bedroom apartment. Leaving Robert, the

house in Hillstem. "Craig do you remember the house Robert had in Hillstem? It was a double story house. Four bedrooms, two bathrooms. Much bigger than our 3 bedroom house. Did I tell you that a month after you returned from university. Robert went off to the city college in Hillstem to study architecture? And it was there that he met a young student from NSW."

- Craig, proudly stated. "That was Vanessa wasn't it?"
- "Yes Vanessa Burns, she was studying to be an accountant." After being there only 6months. Vanessa asked Robert to escort her to a dance on campus.
- [Laughs] "I remember them speaking about the dance." As I recall, If you asked Robert why? He said. "I always knew she liked me." And if you asked Vanessa, why? She said "it's because he was the tallest."

Logan continued, "Their relationship has done nothing but flourish ever since. They moved in together. All that space for two people. When Christmas came around, they invited some friends and family to stay with them. It began to look as if their house isn't actually big enough. Robert's cousin Phillip, parked his caravan in their front yard. All the kids worked together and pitched some tents in the backyard. Robert and Vanessa had their friends trying to convince them of how they should begin a family of their own. Though no one knew just how accurate that suggestion was.

"Just the week before everyone arrived. Vanessa learned that she is pregnant. She has been trying to find the right moment to announce this happy news to Robert. But being busy of late, the moment just hadn't presented itself. Vanessa believes, when she finally gets to tell Robert their happy news. There might be a wedding in their near future?"

Chapter Five

Logan first meeting Robert Evans

Logan, asked Craig. "Please join me for a ride about the grounds." Logan mounted 'Stallion' and Craig got up onto 'Chester'. Craig got Chester when he was 10. Chester is light brown, dark brown hair can be seen in his mane, tail and three of his boots. One resembles fudge, darker than yellow yet not as light as caramel. Although he wasn't that old. Chester had some white to greyish hairs just at the base of his neck. Which is how the name Chester stuck. A young Craig, ran up to family, class mates. Proudly telling anyone who would listen "You must see my horses chess....., his chesitar. Um, I mean his cheshair." People may have just been being polite. Or, they weren't really paying attention to him. Because each replied. "Chester, what a cute name." First they rode along the bank of the billabong, then along the feed route. Stopped and admired the windmill. Stretch their necks looking up at the height of the 15 oak trees in a straight line, down the back of the farm. They then throw some feed around for the chickens and head back toward the garage to put their horses away. Then they sit down on the bench together opposite the turning circle. Logan then said "Let me tell you when I met Robert Evans. Logan sighs, I remember it was afternoon, the year was 1979. You were 4, Robert was 5. You two used to play soccer together in his backyard. Do you remember that? I don't recall exactly how often you played? Some afternoons, he'd just wander over here randomly. This one Saturday he found me out in our garage."

- Robert looked up at me and so politely asked "what ya making?"
- "This door, for the kitchen at our farm 'Winter Forth."
- Robert, [Hands in his pockets, swaying side to side] Politely asks "can I help. Mr Wint?, Mr Winner?"
- I laughed and said, "It's Winter. Ok put your hands here on this wood. Hold them. Good." Robert then accidentally caught the wood with his sleeve and it fell off the table.
- "Sorry, sorry Mr Winter"
- "It's ok my boy," Logan soothed. [picked up the wood and placed it back on the table] Show me your hands, put them here on top of mine."
- "Like this?"
- "No, right here!" said Logan and placed his hands on the wood to show him.
- "Like this Mr Winter?"
- "Yep, that's great mate. Stay there, good. Here's the clip. Ok you can move your hands. Thanks boy."

Logan laughed, "Robert was so polite, intuitive. And has been a reliable assistant whenever I've needed, ever since"

February 10th 1996. 'The oak expedition.'

6 days ago, Craig turned 21. He was outside feeding 'Chester' whom he just rode around the farm on. Back inside, his father Logan saw Craig sitting at the kitchen table. For the size of the manor you'd imagine a large kitchen. It's really not. There is a floor to ceiling walk in pantry, located by a woodstove. [in active] No overhead

cupboards, fully tiled, a double sink. Two windows above the sink. Two more above the small round kitchen table. To the right of table is a doorway to the lounge/sitting room. Directly opposite, left of the fridge is an arch which meets a carpeted hallway down to the office and back door. From the back veranda you then walk over to the laundry room. To the left of the back door is a downstairs toilet. In the kitchen, just back from the sink is a middle bench. Craig has personally knocked into it a few times. But his mum Renee, insists 'it's my prep/serving area'. If anyone were to walk straight through the kitchen door from front veranda. They'd find themselves in the sunroom, it features a coffee table, sofa, two armchairs and beautiful floor to ceiling bay window. That lets the glorious moonlight shine through and warming sun during the day. From there you can head up the two floor stair case. Logan sat down beside him and said. "My son, I will be leaving early, Monday morning for Runegate, QLD. How would you like to accompany me?" Craig was thrilled. And happily accepted. Dad often makes these trips with his business partner Frank Murphy." Together we'll be sourcing out some of the biggest and roundest trees. During our trip, we will visit local shows and markets and catch up with clients local to the area. [Monday, the 12th] The company that Logan owns 'Winter Timber Traders and Son's.' always assigns them a personal travel coordinator. This person organises all their accommodation, local places they can dine at. And plans a travel schedule. Which includes any/all upcoming appointments. They'll stay in Runegate for five days, then travel onto NSW. They'll be in NSW for two-three days then return home to 'Winter Forth.' [9am] Craig and Logan, arrive in Runegate just as the phone begin to ring. Logan was Informed, they need to head straight to the local café. Where they'll be met by their coordinator. Logan reads the paper, while waiting for their coffee to arrive. Craig remained quiet, thinking to himself. "I'm enjoying being here alongside my dad. But I'm also wrestling with a strong desire to return to 'Winter Forth.' He's most eager to be present when the large shipment of pine trees ordered arrives. The aroma from them is not only amazing but the visions and imagining what each log could become is inspiring. A woman approaches their table.

- "Mr Winter? Hello, I'm Helen McKenzie. The company has assigned me to be your personal coordinator." [shakes hand]
- "Nice to meet you, Miss...? Ah. Mrs?" Stammers Logan.
- "Miss McKenzie, but please call me Helen."
- "Helen, please join us. We've just ordered a coffee. May we .... Oh. I see you have one. Maybe something to eat then?" Offers Logan.
- "I'm fine thank you. And who is this with you? A colleague? Business partner?"
- [laughs] "This is my eldest son, Craig." [shakes hands, smiles]
- Helen paused for a moment. Then said "pleased to meet you both. When you're ready, I'll take you to your Hotel. You can get settled and there we'll go over the afternoon schedule."

Helen will soon be 22, she is short. Has medium, straight brown hair and blue eyes. She's been working with the company for near three years. Helen began as a secretary. One month after graduating high school, she was 18. Six months ago, Helen received a promotion to 'Liaison officer'. With this title, came a raise, company car, corporate discount card [widely accepted for goods, services and hotels] It even offered more one on one client based relationships. Craig and Logan were her first non-local clients. Logan was the company owner and honestly Helen's client. But to observe, this instant chemistry between Helen and Craig. You would think they've known each other for two years instead of two hours. Laughing at the same time, finishing each other's sentences. Helen talked about a dream she always had of 'making over her very own kitchen' just like the designs she sees in 'Home décor' monthly editions. Craig, the gentlemen he is. Didn't boast or make fun he just listened. A typical work day, ends at 5pm. Helen left that night at 10pm. Logan knew when he settled down at 8pm. 'my boy is smitten' he [chuckled] then rolled over. Eight days later when they had returned home to 'Winter Forth' Logan realized, he'd accidentally left a suit in the wardrobe of the hotel they stayed at in Runegate. He called Helen. Who said "Mr Winter, I was just about to call you. I just picked up your [they said together, they giggle] 'grey suit!' Craig walked into the kitchen from the front veranda just as

- Logan replies "Thanks Helen, I'll head back there tomorrow morning and pick up my suit. See you then." Logan hung up the phone. He then walked down to the sunroom to let Renee know.

Craig enthusiastically, came running in through the door way.

- "What is it my boy?, I need to speak with your mother!"
- "It's ok dad, I'll go."
- "Ok, Craig. Let me finish speaking with your mother then we can leave after - Logan barely finished.
- Craig assured his father "I've got this dad. I'll be fine by myself."

Craig believed his independent approach would demonstrate assistance, willingness and impression. His parents, Logan and Renee weren't born yesterday. They're much more clever than that. It was obvious so obvious, Craig hasn't been able to think on much else at all. Logan concluded, "He wasn't being helpful! He was going to catch up with Helen." During the next few months. Craig began making more of these 'necessary' trips as he called them to Runegate. They were clearly out of his way and he was neglecting his duties on the farm but Craig was insistent, he missed Helen McKenzie. After the real reason, picking up dad's suit. Each trip, he kept disguising his true desire first with an 'apparently dad forgot to get this signed!' next, it was a 'would you believe it? This is for you, dad, didn't mail your cheque.' Depending on his arrival or departure time amidst all this "urgency" there was conveniently time for a trip to the movies, a beach day or a picnic in the park. [imagine that!] One sunny October morning. Craig and Helen are having breakfast at the 'Rune Café.' When Craig suddenly stood up and announced. "YES!, I'd love to be your boyfriend." Helen, embarrassed by Craig's outcry. Instantly noticed, everyone in the café was now staring at him. Helen, looked straight up at him and nicely said.

- "sit down Craig," Helen leaned in closer to Craig, soothing 8 months, 8 months Craig. I've known and worked with you and your father. I've also heard from other coordinators in our sister branches. "That Logan Winter is a valued and responsible client. [Craig hung his head down, listening] He's never forgotten a phone number, an email address, a mailing address, or a fax number."
- Craig, looked up and said. "It's true!... He sent me to ...."
- Helen said "let me finish. He's not forgotten to sign or properly file documents before leaving town. "Actually he's reminded me of personal dates. I'd made outside of work. Helen [laughs] in fact If he didn't tell me when I spoke to him last week 'don't forget about your mother, 4:00 o'clock.' She'd probably still be at the train station-"
- Craig interrupts but "I..., I mean...., that I ....."
- Helen, smiled placed her hands on either side of his face and said "Ssh! Listen. You have turned up here most urgently stating 'dad forgot, or could you please do this for Logan?

won't you...? [softly] "I'm not silly! A woman knows. I feel something between us too and I have from the moment we met. [Chuckles] Why do you think I agreed to those picnics, or cleared my afternoons. "Even when you 'couldn't' find the paperwork that must be signed! she took his hands Craig, would you be my boyfriend?"

- "Yes! I'd love to" Craig said joyfully.

Craig enjoyed her company more and more. Each visit he felt like shouting out loud "Wow! This is her." Hmm? Just like my Granddad Charlie said. What now...? Oh yeah. That's right. I'd better not let her get away. That's it. Craig truly felt the time has come. Where he's no longer satisfied to just catch up. He wants to be with her. He then pondered, how can I do this though? She works here, her family is here, her friends. I guess there's no harm in asking. She could work in Hillstem just as easily. Then creativity struck, Craig developed a plan. Before he left Runegate he dropped into the real estate agency. After taking a brief tour, he bought a house. Then said to himself. This is going to be great! When I come back with dad in 2months time. I'll have Helen meet me at ...... Instead of at her office like usual. [Two months later] Helen is in her office. She looked up at the clock, notices It's 10:30am and thought to herself. At this rate there'll be no time for coffee. We'll have to check in at the hotel first. "Where are they?" She said, wondering. Helen decided to call Craig's mobile........ [No answer] so she tried his home number [ringing]

- "Hello, 'Winter Forth.' This is Wilson Winter. How may I help you?"
- "Oh, hi Wilson, it's Helen McKenzie."
- "Helen dear, my dad has told me all about you. Their personal travel coordinator. My brother Craig has also fondly talked about you."

- "That's actually why im calling. Wilson, Im looking for your brother. May I ask do you know if Craig got away ok this morning? Cause he hasn't arrived here yet!"
- "Oh, yes. He left here ok. Where are you?"
- "I'm at my office."
- "Oh, Helen. My goodness. That's my bad! I was the one who was meant to call you last night. Craig, left a message with me knowing he wouldn't have time in the morning. "I'm so sorry, I forgot all about it. Hang on dear, let me just [rustling through papers] yeah, here it is. [reading aloud] "Wilson please call Helen [Chuckles], continues. And let her know that instead of meeting me at her office. Could she please meet me, 11:30am at 14 Buckingham Street. Love Craig. That's all it says Helen. Sorry I couldn't be of more help. And I apologize again for not phoning you last night."
- "That's ok Wilson, ooh! 10:45 now. 11.30? That doesn't give me much time! I'd better get going. Thank you and goodbye Wilson."
- "Bye dear."

Helen, leaves her office and hails a taxi. She then thinks. Buckingham Street? That's about 15minutes from here. I should just make it. Helen soothed. Helen grew up in Runegate and admittedly knows the area really well. {Thinking} that address, how do I know it? she asked herself.... Then it came to her, It's a house for sale.

Chapter Six

11th of December 1996, Will you live with me?

S tanding near the mail box. Helen looked around at the brick house in front of her. It was fully fenced, it had a single car garage small white pebbles around the garden beds. A carport. A split concrete path leading up to it. Helen is puzzled, she begins to wonder this is a residential area. Not business. Im at a house, not an office. She then says out loud "Just what could that man be up to?" This street, address. Buckingham Street? Last year, two colleagues of mine from work looked into purchasing this house together. That's why it sounds so familiar. Her friends described it as the perfect two bedroom house, close to work, within walking distance to the mall. Helen knocked on the door, no answer. At the door, Helen called out "hello...?" no answer. She tried the handle, it wasn't locked, so she went in. At the end of the hall, Helen's gaze was automatically drawn to the most beautifully designed beige kitchen she'd ever seen. She could hardly believe it! Helen said to herself could this really be the same house her friends Cindy and Kerri passed on? She then soothed, No. Helen you're being silly. It can't be! According to them it needed repairs to the kitchen and lounge room floor and some of the window trims needed mending. Hearing this in her head. Helen then thought..... Well Craig is a qualified carpenter. Walking around the house, Helen noticed some other moved in items. Two suitcases, a box on the kitchen bench, a small square wooden dining table, 3 seater lounge, two towels in the bathroom and a couple of toothbrushes.

- [door opens] *"Honey, im home.* Craig said playfully. He then asked "what do you think?"
- Extremely puzzled right now. But Helen answered, "I think it looks very cosy for two people. Helen then asked "so when is Russell moving in?"
- "Russell?" replied Craig. With a question in his voice as to who he is? "Oh my business partner Russell. [laughs] Craig then says "no. Guess again."
- "I know, I've got it. This is where your mum stays when she accompanies your dad, while working.'
- "No, [chuckles] let me explain. Actually, I'll show you."

He instructed Helen to close her eyes and take his hand. [She obeyed] "Now, no peeking walk with me just through here. Hold on! Not yet!, Craig opens the curtains "Ok, you can open them." He then walked over to the right side of the beautifully made double bed opened the top bedside drawer. Motioned to Helen then said

- "This bedside table and the dresser over there are for you. Oh, oh and one full side of this [opens double doors] our wardrobe. I know you'd love to just go wild, incorporate those tips/suggestions you so fondly read about in your monthly home décor magazines."
- Helen excitedly said to Craig. "Our wardrobe, our lounge our beautiful kitchen. Is this your unique way of asking me to move in with you?"
- "Yes," replied Craig. He reached out and took Helen's hands and said "These last 10months with you have been the

happiest of my life and I can't imagine spending the next 10seconds without you by my side."

- "That's so sweet Craig." She leans into him and they hug each other and kiss. Places that come together this wonderfully only exist in peoples dreams. I couldn't have imagined our place any differently." and they kiss again.
- Craig said "hey!, Do you always kiss men in strange houses? Or is that an acceptance?"
- "Yes." smiles Helen.
- Craig looked at her concerned. "Yes to which question?"
- [giggles] "Yes, it's an acceptance. I'd love to move in with you, I love you Craig Winter."
- "I love you too Helen McKenzie."[hug and kiss]

That afternoon, after work Helen begins moving in. Although it is only for five days as they're scheduled to return to Winter Forth. That time spent in their new house were the most memorable days they'd ever had together. [Winter Forth Farm]

Mrs Sherwood stood at the bottom of the front steps, eagerly awaiting to greet Craig and Helen, who've just pulled up next to the garage. Craig got their bags from the boot of the car and sat them on the veranda. Mrs Sherwood helped carry them into the sitting room. Craig walked down the hallway and out onto the back veranda. He stood there quietly, Helen joined him soon after and said.

- "Dear, Meredith is asking if you'd like a coffee?"
- "Not just now thank you. I'm gonna stay out here for a bit. Call out if you need any help at all"

looking out over the grounds of the farm. Craig laughed and smiled then suddenly begun [reminiscing] A flood of childhood memories suddenly become vivid. As if they were happening, right now all over again. He saw himself running along the billabong, using squirt guns on his recently hung out school uniforms, running around playing fetch with their dog 'Angus.' Driving lessons with dad along the feed route. The veranda was on the ground floor. With the happy memories also came some sad times, painful falls and fights with Wilson. Craig laughed as he watched afternoons where he'd chased Wilson around their front garden. Memories then re-surfaced, mapping out the final resting places of beloved pets. But mostly happy memories. Chuckles, closed his eyes. Now he can see. One afternoon when his mum Renee was out at by the clothes line. And he recklessly galloped by riding 'Chester'

- Mum [called out] "Craig, slow down! Dust is sweeping over all my clean laundry.'
- "YEees Muuum!" loud at first and fainter as he rode further away.

[present] Craig then felt a familiar overwhelming feeling. It again suggested to him he should settle down and begin a family of his own. Craig believes it most likely originated from seeing how happy his parents/grandparents are together. He glanced out over the grounds again. Only this time he was swarmed with the images of what his own children would be like? Games they'd play, pets they'd own. How they'd run up to him for a hug after school. Craig took in a deep breath then let it out, and pondered the question out loud. Will 'Winter Forth' be a big enough place after all?" These last few years, before he'd met Helen. Craig felt this ache, an unbearable loneliness. He never envisioned himself falling in love but each day they spend together is always much better than their yesterday. Craig walked back inside and sat down in the sitting room. Helen came and sat beside him.

- Craig told Helen, "Just now when I was outside. I noticed that the manor and the grounds need minor renovations."
- Helen added, "usually your dad does the work around here right?"
- "Yes, but since the accident 7 months ago whilst he was riding 'Stallion' he has been unable to do much heavy work."

Mrs Sherwood then said, "Logan was left with severe bruising. And minor damage to his lower back. Moving, even minimal has become slower for him of late. "Wilson has been taking care of 'Winter Forth' I meant to call you when it happened. Your parents temporarily moved into a one bedroom house in Hillstem. "Mrs Winter was here yesterday. I asked her, if I should let you know? All I got told was. We'll call him!"

- "yes, it's all good Meredith. They sent me a message. We are arranging to catch up soon. Hey Meredith, do you know if they're renting the house in Hillstem?"
- "No, they bought one. Your mother, Renee believed that a single story home would be better for Logan's rest and recovery. Meredith continued, I know Mr Winter dislikes having to rely on Renee so much. "Not being able to get about as efficiently as he once did. You know my boy, how stubborn and independent he's always been.
  'much like his own mother' in that regard!"
- "Fortunately for us Craig is more than capable of carrying out these renovations."
- "And Frank Murphy, can handle things at work with the regular clients?" Craig continued "If necessary, I can call Russell or Robert to help me. They'd be happy to lend us a hand. Craig then thought to himself. [oh darn] Robert is away at the moment."

- Mrs Sherwood asked, "Can I get either of you anything to eat? I cooked up some sausages, bacon, eggs and some hash browns."
- "Ooh! You made hash browns?, with your home-made tomato sauce?" Asked Craig hopefully.
- Meredith laughed then replied "no, they were frozen."
- "Were all good thank you, Meredith. We're gonna go and unpack."

Craig said. "I'll call Russell tomorrow arvo, he'll help us. Should be done in about 2-3 weeks or so, I imagine. Like I said, they're only minor. "First task; repairing the back steps. Next; mending some of the kitchen cabinets. Umm? I think that was all…. Oh yeah wait, build a stand for mums new small water tank for the laundry. "And lastly a reconstruction of the edge of the fishing dock that runs along our billabong." Craig hesitated in contacting Russell, after moving to the town of Hillstem. He wasn't sure how keen he'd be to return and or help out? But when he turned up it surprised him. Russell looked over the list Craig made. Russell wrote something down then handed it back to Craig. He then walked over to his car to grab his tool box. Russell then announced. "Come on guys, today we're in the kitchen." Craig reviewed Russell's notes, turned to say "This looks good mate." But Russell wasn't there! He must have quickly ducked back inside to grab a drink. On my way back inside to look for him. I called out to Wilson, who was halfway down the driveway.

- "Come back inside!," No response, I called again "Wilson, we're working inside today!," No response. I repeated, louder this time. "Wilson, come on bro! We're working inside today!" still nothing.

I walked over to him. As I got closer, I noticed Wilson staring up at the line of oak trees on the right hand side. I shook his shoulder and said. "Wilson!"

- He turned to me and said, "yeah?"
- I asked him "Are you alright mate? What just happen? Where were you just now?"
- Wilson said. "Craig, do you remember this row of trees?" [pointing along them]
- Craig sarcastically responded "Yeah! The ones we planted!"
- Wilson, [laughing] "It's hard to believe isn't it? That they were once small, seedlings in their pots."
- Craig sternly said, "Small! Huh? Those pots, didn't seem so small or light! The time we lugged all 10 of them over here from the back shed." Craig [giggled] then continued. "I don't remember exactly when it was. Though I do remember being grateful it was a cool afternoon. And how eventually we loved the shade those trees provided us while waiting for the school bus."
- You know, said Wilson. "I always believed that Dad came up with that idea as a form of punishment. Because whenever I or you talked back or neglected our chores. We were given tasks to do just like that."
- Craig replied, "Thinking back on it now, I realise it wasn't such a bad thing, having to spend time outdoors.
- "Yeah, though at the time. it felt like a punishment." Said Wilson.

Tuesday the 8th of April 1997.

It's been just over a year now since Craig met Helen and when they're weren't travelling around for work, their spare time was spent at 'Winter Forth.' They still own the house in Runegate. Which, is usually rented out. Craig walked into the kitchen, sat down at the table and called Russell.

- 'Thompson,' Russell speaking, "how might I help you?"
- "Hi mate, it's Craig. Listen I appreciated your being here assisting us with the renovations. But I wonder if you could do me another favour?"
- "What's that mate?"
- "I need you to fill in full time for me with the business? As well as be of assistance to Mrs Sherwood around 'Winter Forth' when necessary. I've organized a special two week trip for Helen and I."
- "Please tell Helen, it will be my pleasure to help out. Where are you going?"
- "Paris, Craig said happily. Helen has always wished to see the Eiffel Tower, take a tour of the museums and visit as many art galleries as time allows."
- "Wow! That sounds wonderful, Im sure you'll have a great time. We have some happy news ourselves. Cherry and I have picked September. To get married.
- "That's wonderful, Russell. This year, right?"
- "Yep! Exact day, TBA." Then adds, "your trip sounds amazing, am sure you'll have a great time mate. Let me speak to Helen, I wanna wish her a great time too."

"Ssh! No! Silly! I can't tell her yet. It's a surprise trip! "Helen has been itching to return to work. I'm sure she's suspected something these past few days when I haven't allowed her to leave! "I'm hoping she continues to buy my repetitive 'I just need your help with this my love.' Statement."

- "When are you leaving?"

- "We leave next Tuesday morning. Thanks for this Russell. I can hardly wait. You would know better than anyone. What Helen means to me. From that moment I first saw Helen McKenzie. I felt my life would never be the same again!"
- "I'll come over early and drive you to the airport." Offered Russell.
- "That will be helpful, thanks again. Catch ya later mate."
- 'you're welcome, Craig. I'll see you Tuesday. Bye."

After getting off the phone, Russell thought to himself. My fiancé Cheryl Williams leaves Monday morning. Russell's partner, Cheryl. Has asked us all to call her [Cherry] is a romance novelist. Professionally known as 'Cherry Rose Blossom.' Cherry, became well recognised a year and a half ago. Following the release of her debut book. Entitled 'I do, give an ass!' according to her it is and I quote 'made up!' Personally, I believe it relates to her roommate Chloe, Elizabeth. Whom she roomed with 6 years at boarding school. Cherry, neither confirms or denies my accusations. Russell picks up a copy of the book and reads the back cover aloud.

> "A passionate, determined 47 yr old woman, feels it's her destiny to be a travelling free spirit. Along her journey her confidence shines as bright as all her cheeks. Eliza lived most of her life for someone else. Now newly single has decided to seek out herself and finally ask these two questions. 1) what do I like? 2) What do I need? Weeks of awaiting answers. Nothing, no clarity. Until one morning.... She stood in front of her mirror and called out her questions. Eliza and her cat, are the only ears. A voice answers her. Success! She has it "Eliza, you've always been headstrong and focused in your professional everyday life. Owning each room you walk into." Her cat 'Diddles', (looks up. Meows, licks lips.) In agreement. Hearing this out loud. Eliza now knows. When it comes to

passion, intimacy. 'She secretly desires her partner to take dominance, owning their room." Cherry Rose Blossom.

For the following two months, Cherry will be travelling in and around Europe [book tour] promoting the release of her latest novel 'Swing set swingers' Russell, convinced their house will feel so lonely and be so quiet without her around. Is happy to help Helen and Craig out. Ever since moving to the city, Russell has longed for the country life once again. Tending to a farm, riding around on horses, swimming. Ah, well when there isn't work to be done, of course. Plus he'll get to see, Mrs Sherwood again.

Chapter Seven

15th of April 1997, Our trip to Paris

Roughly 23 hours later, Craig and Helen have arrived in Paris. They collect their bags then make their way toward the front entrance, hoping to hail a taxi to their hotel. Now checked in, they get changed and decide to go on a breathtaking walk through the nearby park. Walking along, hand in hand. Helen remarks at how beautiful the scenery is in. There's an outdoor stage area lined with garden beds, featuring a variety of colourful flowers. A medium size kids play area over to the left. Helen then asked Craig

- "Can you imagine how beautiful this area is decorated for events like Christmas, concerts and or celebrations?"
- "I'll bet it's beautiful, he then asked "Do you remember that old saying 'so much to see, so little time?"
- "I do, and your right. So in that case. I'd suggest tomorrow we go sightseeing. Visit some local markets, art studios. We can even take a train ride."

After researching, there is only one local train tour. Which travels out to.....? Yes, it takes you on a tour. Then it travels out to a museum called 'Old Tramway.' Which has old trams and out dated trains on display. There was wonderful sights, and attractions viewed along the way. At 'Old Tramway' they also run their own tour. Craig and Helen just walked around, exploring at their own pace. One interactive feature there, intrigued them both it was called '20 miles in the 20's.' There you could choose from a wondrous variety of costumes, and props. You then have your photograph taken appearing like a couple or family ranging from the late 1920's right up until the early 1980's. Craig joked about them being on the cover for our 80's rock band. If Helen, hadn't of laughed it off. I've no doubt that Craig would have found them matching punk style wigs. Luckily, Craig moved onto inspecting the wall of portraits, from previous visitors. Helen tried to convince Craig, that we should do this. Telling him 'it'll be something for "just us."

- Craig asked, "what if our children, wish to see it? Or our friends? What shall we tell them?"
- "nothing!, we just simply say, "sorry, it's private!"

Craig didn't respond. He just returned to the walls of portraits. Helen began skimming through the clothes rack. She was most excited to find two particular outfits. Helen got Craig's attention, then held them up, side by side for him to see. Craig returned to her. Now beside her.

- Helen leaned into Craig's shoulder and seductively said. "You'd make the perfect Clyde to my Bonnieee," Helen then pointed to the gun rack on the back wall. "However, we'll need one more thing each."
- Craig [laughed] and replied "I just saw a portrait around the corner. And I have my own scene idea, if you don't mind?, Give me a moment."

Craig approached the photographer. Though brief, their chat was so soft. Helen unfortunately couldn't make out what it was.

When they returned to their hotel that afternoon. They were both treated to a relaxing in room Massage. Now feeling all relaxed and refreshed, Craig opened a bottle of wine, poured out two glasses. Handed one to Helen, then nestled down beside her on the two seater lounge.

- "Cheers my darling." they each took a sip. Then Craig, set his glass down on the side table. He then took Helen's glass out of her hand and placed it down beside his. Craig Leaned in, kissed Helen and said. "You know something?, You are the most beautiful woman in Paris!"
- Helen, [giggles] "really, I don't know about that Mr Winter. But I do know, I'm one of the luckiest women in Paris to be here with you." [They kiss each other] and have some more wine.
- Craig than asked Helen, "would you do me the honour of having dinner with me tomorrow evening?"
- "It would be my pleasure, Mr Winter."

[Tomorrow evening] 'Come on Honey, the driver will be out the front any minute' called Craig. "Alright, I'm on my way." She calls back. Helen stood near the door. Craig looked Helen up and down, hmm? A handbag on your left arm and a....?

- "Is that a single short stemmed, red rose in your right hand?, Craig asked. [Puzzled] then said "ah, wha? Well, um. It's pretty."
- Helen smiled "It's for your jacket."

When they walked into the restaurant they were greeted by a very pleasant young lady who asked "may I help you?' Craig simply replied "Winter, 7pm for two." Upon hearing this Helen began thinking to herself was this a plan? Could he have made a booking?

She then continued reasoning within her mind. No, he couldn't have! We were literally just driving by down on the street. When Craig suddenly announced "how about this one?, I'll bet it will have an amazing view up there." That man of mine is just full of surprises.

- The stewardess replied "very good sir, please wait through there and an usher will soon walk you to your table." Helen, who still looked mesmerized by all this, smiled.
- Craig took her hand, kissed it and says "you know, I love you?"
- she [blushed, kissed him on the lips] and replied "yes, I love you too my dear."

This restaurant is on the third level of a four level building. Fourth level is the roof and some small store rooms. The three levels feature an elegant gold staircase and glass elevators. Parking is at ground level. Level one is a cafeteria. Level two is an art gallery which according to their brochures. Many pieces of artwork, sculptures, murals and mosaics created by talented local artists. Are prominently on display throughout the restaurant. Some are even for sale. On the balcony of the restaurant there is a small round garden, a D.O.S.A (designated outdoor smoking area) and a small fountain. A man approached them [French accent] "good evening, Sir, Madame. I'm Marcus, if you'll plez follow me, your tabel [pointing left] iz a ziz way." Craig took Helen's hand and they followed in behind Marcus who led them to a table by the window. Along the way, Helen became mesmerized by one of the biggest, shiniest chandeliers. That hung in the middle of the dining room. [flicking through her home décor magazines.] Helen has seen such beauty. But never up close. "Please, madam." said Marcus motioning to Helen as he pulled out her chair "thank you" Helen replied, then sat. Their window showed a stunning view of the Eifel Tower. It was absolutely beautiful. Each window appeared to offer a 'great view' but Helen believed theirs to be the most 'amazing view of them all'. Hmm. [just as Craig had imagined] Marcus handed them each a menu. And told them "your Matre D will be with you shortly. In the meantime, could I get either of you a drink?" 'Craig replied, "Just a bottle of white wine please." "Oui Sir, I hope you both enjoy your evening." Said Marcus.

Chapter Eight

------- ❦ -------

The proposal

"Good evening, Sir, Ma'am. I'm Phillipe and I'll be your waiter this evening. Are you ready to place your order?"

- "Yes answered Craig, for our entrée we'd like your 'puff pastry wreath and brie.' And for our main meal we'll both have the 'smoked salmon, with mashed potatoes and vegetables.' Thank you Phillipe."
- "Oui Sir."
- "Craig, this meal was delicious."
- "'I'm pleased you liked it." Craig than raised his hand straight up into the air, motioning Phillipe to come to their table.
- "How may I help you, sir?" asked Phillipe.
- "We'd like to order our dessert please."
- "Oui Sir, might I recommend our -"
- "Craig interrupted, It's ok. My lovely lady would like the crème brulee. As for me..... [reading] hmm? I'll have a chocolate éclair with whipped cream on the side. Oh and Phillipe, I'll also have the 'special' too."
- "Oui sir."

Phillipe stood up, immediately removed his apron and rapidly twirled it around above his head. Within seconds, Marcus appeared at our table and placed down a gift in front of Helen. He topped up their wine. Then stood off to one side. Helen, carefully unwrapped her gift which was nestled in the middle of a silver plate. She reached in and pulled out a small wooden chest. Immediately noticed Craig's handy work. Helen examined it. Yes the style, the carvings. She remembered last year Craig designed near 50 of these for a client. [a hens night] Helen [blushing] looked up at Craig, who smiled back at her. She lifted up the lid of the chest, reached in and pulled out a ring. [sighing] It was just gorgeous. A gold band with an opal in the middle.

- Helen [put her hands to her face) then cried out excitedly. "Yes!, I will marry you Craig!"
- Craig [surprised] stood up and announced. "Mind if I ask the question first?"
- [Helen giggled] Craig, knelt down on one knee in front of Helen and Asked "Helen Patricia McKenzie, will you do me the honour of becoming my wife?" He then placed the ring onto her finger. Helen then held her hand up to admire it and she happily replied
- "Yes, Craig Daniel Winter, I will be your wife."

They stood up together [hugged and kissed] everyone within close proximity to their table cheered out in celebration and congratulations, whilst [raising] up their glasses. Craig took Helen's arm and said "let's go home." Along the drive back to their Hotel. Helen, just couldn't help wondering again. How did Craig know his way around the restaurant? He asked for the 'special', told me where the restroom was. Did he actually arrange it all? Ok Helen thought. For arguments sake, even if it was true he planned it. The more interesting question was when? or how? After careful consideration. Helen submitted and soothed. This only re affirms what I've felt and known for some time now. [sighs] quote 'That man of mine is full of surprises.' We've set our wedding date for 6 months from now. To take place in Runegate, many of my friends, family and colleagues still reside there. Back at 'Winter Forth' everyone was happy to hear of Craig and Helen's engagement. There was mention of a souvenir portrait. Yet to date. None other than Craig or Helen have seen it.

Chapter Nine

The wedding dress

Two weeks later, Helen went out shopping with her best friend Lydia. As Lydia was Maid of honour. She was keen to get started with bachelorette planning. They passed a bank of shops before entering the mall. One of them was a bridal shop. On display in the window, Helen saw the most amazing wedding dress and she instantly fell in love with it.

- "I see you eyeing that up. You should try it on." Encouraged Lydia.
- 'No, shops like these only have the ones on display. They don't keep different sizes available."
- "Well you won't know my dear, unless you ask, you'll never know!"
- "Your right my dear, let's go in."

When inside, Helen headed straight over to the dress in the window and felt the material, which is every bit as smooth and silky as she believed it would be. She then noticed the size. "Oh no! see I told you. The tag says, 12, I need a 14."

- "We can ask them. Look the sales lady is standing right there. They may order you one. Here come with me." Lydia took Helen by the hand and they walked up to the counter together.

- The sales woman asked "may I help you ladies?"
- Helen hesitated, then said. 'Everything is fine, we're good......, I just hoped -"
- Lydia firmly interrupted. "Yes, my friend here wishes to try that dress on. [Pointing to the one on display] only can we please have the size 14?"
- "Give me a moment, it will be in the back. Within minutes the sales woman returned and said 'we found it, our fitting rooms are just back there behind the mirrors, then to your left. "My name is Crystal, If you'll excuse me? I've got a few things to be getting on with. I'd like to leave you in the capable hands of my assistant. "Elizabeth. If you make your way to the dressing room, Elizabeth will bring the dress in to you. And she will be able to assist you further okay?"
- That's fine with us, thank you. Stated Helen. She then walked down to the dressing room.
- [knocking] "its Elizabeth dear, here's your dress.
- 5mins later, Elizabeth [knocks again] and asks "how is it going Miss?"
- "Ugh! Struggling, not so good! replied a worried Helen. She then asked Liz, if she'd "bring her the next size please?"
- "Sure, I won't be long, honey." 2 minutes later. Elizabeth returned and said "here you are, I'll be right out here if you need me."

[5 mins later] Helen emerged from the dressing room. Wearing the same clothes she had on when she first walked in there. We each expected to see a radiant, ecstatic bride to be before us. Although she was blushing. Helen marched up to the counter, placed down the two dresses and politely said.

- "Thank you for all your help Liz. Unfortunately the '16' didn't fit either. We must go. We have a hair appointment coming up. But I'd like to drop back by this afternoon. To try on the size 18!"
- Crystal, overhearing returned to the counter. "Oh dear, I'm so sorry we only have these two sizes in stock. We're happy to order one in for you. Shouldn't take more than a week."
- "That'll be great." Replied Helen.
- "I'll book a personal fitting for you and give you a call when your dress has arrived. Enjoy the rest of your afternoon ladies."
- "Thanks heaps Elizabeth, I appreciate that"

Outside Lydia suggested Helen sit on a nearby bench, while she ducks in next door to grab them a cup of coffee. Helen reminds her, "don't be too long! They still need to get to the salon." Lydia assured, "I'll be right back." As Helen watched her enter the 'Coffee cup' She began thinking back on just how good a friend, Lydia Murray has been to her. Good old Lydia. Helen just didn't know how she ever would have gotten through high school without her? Lydia is not only an amazing women. She's a terrific friend. Helen never had to worry about anything. Whenever she was upset or stressed about an upcoming test. Her phone would just ring and there she was. Before even say hi or speaking any words at all.

Lydia sighed and asked, "oh dear, what did they say this time? And which one was it? Or she said don't worry, you'll do better next time." She knew, she always knew. Helen always got teased for being the shy girl. Never talked back or stood up for herself. Lydia was always comforting and supportive when hearing Helen out. Lydia knew who those nasty girls were. Lydia moved to Runegate when she was just 13. Her dad leased a shop front. There he established his own fish and chip shop. Which he called 'Fish n Fry'. Lydia's a year younger than Helen but were in the same grade 8 class. When Lydia was the new girl, no one liked her because she had freckles and wore glasses. But by the end of year 9, Lydia had attracted a circle of friends, all from the grades above us. At lunch times, they all sat together. One afternoon, half way through finishing year 9. Helen was sitting under a tree next to the science lab. Just quietly reading, minding her own business. When two girls from year 11, began making fun of her school skirt. They chanted over and over 'hand me down, hem hanging around!' Mocking Helen, just because her skirt didn't have the same pleats as theirs. Helen put her head down into her shirt and began to cry. Then she heard muffled voices, Helen looked up and found those girls were gone. Lydia knelt down beside her, placed a hand on her shoulder. Still not exactly sure what Lydia said to them? But Mum, Helen has said no one bothered her again after that. New students, tried intimidating her. They'd get right up in her face. Lydia, would look straight at them and say "lo....?, Star...? Best, that's ever been made out is Lydia said the word 'Lobster' then amazingly, whoever they were? Just turned and walked away. One of mum's proudest high school memories. Was when she told me she had tried it on a group of boys, who were making fun of her shoes. Apparently, all they did was laugh. It didn't have the same effect for some reason. There were many times Lydia stood up for Helen. But whatever, whoever or however it happened. Helen was so grateful to have her as her best friend then and every day since. [present] Lydia sat down beside me. Here you go dear and handed me my coffee. I have asked Lydia on more than one occasion. What's with the word 'Lobster?' and each time she puts her hand over my mouth and says Ssh! I can't discuss it. I then wondered if it's because she saw something at her dad's 'Fish N Fry' shop? That she can't repeat. Hmm? Its uncanny, every time I bring it up with her, im thinking that maybe todays the day? After all high school was almost 7 years ago. She's bound to tell me! Yet

I get that same response. Still! Replying 'I can't discuss it!' Just like that. [sighs] Helen takes a sip of her coffee. Turns to Lydia and says

- "I just don't understand what happened at the dress shop? I've always been careful about maintaining a healthy figure. "Hmm? You know? Now that I think of it my favourite jeans were a little snug when I put them on last week. And my favourite shoes. "Well, thank goodness for slip on shoes. Remind me when I get home to make a doctor's appointment"

Four days later. Morning Helen, please sit down. Said Dr Willoughby he then continued. "Helen we have the results from your blood test!"

- "Goodness! Exclaimed Helen, are they ………? I mean, what…?"
- "No, no. Dear. They are fine!' Soothed the doctor. You're seven weeks pregnant."
- "Pregnant, aww. That's wonderful Doc."
- "Helen, I'll need you to drop back sometime next week for an ultrasound."

Outside, Helen gave Craig a call. No answer. Now, driving home to tell Craig the happy news, Helen was positively glowing. When Helen walked in the door she was greeted by Russell who lovingly passed on his 'congratulations' to her. She thought, to me? [how could he possibly know?, I only just got home!]

- Russell hugged her and said "Happy engagement."
- "Oh! Engagement, she laughed. Thanked Russell then asked if he knows where Craig is? He didn't answer his phone."
- "He's over by the garage."

- "Ok, thank you. Russell. I'll just go and see him."

We never officially had an engagement party. Just a family dinner at home. Partially due to us both being unable to get time off work. Naturally Russell will be Craig's best man, Lydia will be my maid of honour. A title I proudly held at Lydia's wedding two years ago when she married interior designer, Joshua Murray. When I told Craig of our happy news. Craig was as excited about it as me. He insisted on returning to the doctor's office with me. While we were waiting I also told Craig about the dress I've fallen in love with. Lydia helped me pick it out. I then went to say "It's just.... That I [hesitating] I won't be....... I'm afraid I ...."

- "What? Afraid of what?"
- "I won't fit into it. [crying a little, sniffs] Not just yet anyway."
- "Ooh, my darling, he soothes. It'll be okay. We'll just postpone our wedding for a bit is all." He takes her hand, kisses it. Then re assures "I promise it will be just as wonderful in May of next year, as a posed to October."

I was relieved, Craig was so understanding. Truthfully, I expected an old fashioned, "sorry, I won't have a child out of wedlock attitude. I know his grandparents are of that mind. Thankfully, Craig isn't."

Doctor Willoughby, said to Helen and Craig. "Come in, you sit there Craig. And you Helen, please lie down up here. And we'll have a listen to your baby's heartbeat." [a few minutes later] Craig and Helen, eagerly listen and view the monitor. Craig leans and hugs Helen. Who asks "How is everything doctor? Is it all normal?"

- 'Perfectly normal, everything looks real good here. Right size and babies heartbeat is strong.' Before you leave, be sure to make a follow up appointment for 4 weeks. And ask my receptionist to put your names down for pre- natal classes. The group meets here fortnightly on a Tuesday afternoons."

- Craig opened the door for Helen and said "thank you Dr Willoughby, see you in a month."

Chapter Ten

---⚜---

Welcome Lucy

Helen's pregnancy progressed really well. All throughout she remained so calm and confident that everything was fine. Efficiency is ensured with one carpenter's work. But this project, lovingly called 'finish the nursery'. Had three brilliant minds. Around the fifth month, Craig and Helen knew they were having a little girl. Craig as the expectant father wrestled with some doubt about finalization. He was assured by his father Logan. "That things will be fine." [no doubt, based on his own experiences] However it was uncle Russell, who became more unglued. He tried to stay positive, but to look at him and listen to him. It almost seemed as if he felt he'd let everyone down if it wasn't completed on time. On one of the expeditions Craig went on with his father Logan. He'd selected a really beautiful oak tree trunk, that in his words was 'drawn to me immediately.' Much like the rocking chair, of '1991.' From the moment the milling began, pieces piled up on the ground. Craig said to himself 'this will make a beautiful crib!' It was the final coat of paint that took the longest to dry. [Lucy] is the name they chose. Was due to be born on the 24th of December. The 24th of December, has since come and gone.... No baby! Dr Willoughby said. "These things can happen, especially with first time pregnancies. Everything appears where it should be. I predict, we meet this little girl in two weeks, give or take." According to Craig. When Helen announced 'false alarm' on the 1st of January. Russell let out a "phew!" As these past few weeks have seen each of them working day and night. To have everything finished before D-Day.

- Craig often told Helen, "he repeated it again today!"
- "you're kidding me?" she laughs.
- "Nope, I saw him. And I heard him, He believed no one was near him, as he washed out the paintbrushes."
- [giggles] Ooh, Craig. Was it the same statement/phrase that he's been singing?" asked Helen intrigued.
- 'Yep! He surely did, I swear to you. I wish, I'd recorded it. Might make a great song or poem one day. "A moment of frustration for Russell to remember. But my goodness! It certainly was catchy."

Russell singing ["if I don't get done, and paint with class.
this young lass,
will sleep in the stable or under the kitchen table.
Gotta finish, gotta paint.
I ain't gonna diminish, this young lasses wish."]

On the 6th of Jan, 1998. 12.15am at Hillstem General Hospital. Lucy Crystal Winter was welcomed into the world. Hair was brown, no noticeable curls. Craig said. "We'll see, they may yet come in." Dad's nose and mum's blue eyes. 52cm long, HCC 54cm and weighing 2702g.

Day before Wedding.

"Come on Craig! We're meant to be there at 2pm. I need to pick up my wedding dress." Said Helen. "Alright let's go. Wilson! We're leaving now!" Said Craig and shut the front door. "I heard from Russell yesterday. That you really do adore the suits you plan on wearing tomorrow. I can't believe it Craig. Our wedding is tomorrow morning. It seems like only yesterday that we moved into our house in Runegate and had that most wonderful trip to Paris. [Sighs] I'm so lucky Craig, to be marrying the love of my life." [They kiss passionately] Helen could just imagine. If Russell walked in and saw them kiss like that he would have said. "hey, mate save some for tomorrow." Laugh, then close the door. Apologizing every step on the way back out.

Wedding day 8th of May 1998.

10am, Helen is standing in the back room of the church with her father Jerry, he moves in closer to his daughter, kisses her on the forehead. "My little girl you are the....., looks around, checking his wife Becky is not close by. The prettiest girl, sorry woman here," he offers his arm to Helen, and says "shall we?" First person to begin walking was Helen's sister Mary whose carrying little flower girl Lucy [4 months old]. Followed closely by pageboy Troy. [Robert and Vanessa Evans son] Beautiful bridesmaids Monique [Wilson's partner] and Cherry [Russell's partner]. Next was the maid of honour, Lydia. Then Helen's mother Becky. The aisles were decorated with freshly picked sunflowers on either side. Along the carpet was a gorgeous mixture of pink, white and red rose petals for Bride Helen to walk upon. Helen thought she would be fighting feelings of nervousness but instead all she felt was happy and content. Helen took her father's arm and began walking in behind the precision. Keeping her eyes fixated on Craig's the entire time. He was standing to the right of groomsmen, Helen thought [Wow! Russell shines up nicely] Best men, Wilson and Robert were standing to the left of Russell. Jerry took his seat next to Becky. Then the minister began the ceremony. Later, the minister concluded with "ladies and gentlemen it gives me great pleasure to introduce Mr and Mrs Winter." Becky crying, everyone else cheered. "I've also been asked to invite you all to join us at the reception being held at the local RSL club."

[3 months later] 'Country Life' Bed and breakfast.

With Helen, unable to return to work at present. Much of her time is spent at 'Winter Forth Farm' with Lucy. Craig works Mon-Fri and makes deliveries on a Saturday until 1pm. Mostly local, depending on order. This weekend though Lucy is spending with Helen's parents, Jerry and Becky. Helen gave Mrs Sherwood the night off. And for dinner, Helen was most excited to prepare a roast beef. However growing up in the city. Helen became comfortable with take away drive thru and eating out. It has just now occurred to her she wasn't exactly sure how to do this. Perhaps it would have been smart to ask Mrs Sherwood before her and Marcus left. Helen tried calling her mother..... no answer. They must have gone out. She called Lydia.... Hoping she could help. Got only her voice mail. She is then struck with a realization. Remembering when she moved in here. She had put some of cook books in the kitchen. Only one problem. Helen couldn't think where in the kitchen. She got down on her knees and began her search. Drawers, no. Bench cupboards, no. Maybe cupboard under the sink? No. None of her things. But Helen did see some books, in the corner cupboard. Wedged up against the right side. Right at the back. 6 old A4 exercise books, in total. Some of which appeared to have loose papers sticking out of them. Helen said Uh-ha, these must be recipe books. I'll use them. She then cleared off the table, placed down the books and began flicking through. Scanning for 'beef' or 'roast'. "Nope, nothing. Helen said. Just a bunch of writing and dates. She read on. This is a table of contents. 1988...... page 1-4, 1989...... page 5-9, 1990..... page 10-14, 1991.... Page 15-19. Helen, turned the page and saw 4 marked out columns. A list of dates was in the first column, next column was titled: income, third column was titled: expenses, last column was titled: total. The last page of the book was a summary. It read; guest total then the number, total income, and total expenses. Also a line entitled Banked by and a signature. All Helen could clearly make out was E. M. Sherwood. Sherwood? She said to herself. I picked up another notebook. Inside the cover of this one was the title: Building supplies, workers and bank repayments. Another book of dates, these begin from 1975. Helen begun asking herself. What are these? She looked around. This manor we live in has two levels, three bedrooms and an office. To my knowledge. I've not seen it used as an office. But it's what everyone calls. The last room at the end of the hallway. I peeked in there once. All I saw was boxes, old children's toys, some old suitcases. And an old pram. No shelves, no filing cabinet. Not even a lamp or desk. Just floor to ceiling boxes. Hmm? Mrs Sherwood is not due back until tomorrow morning. I can't speak to her. I'll call Renee, perhaps she can shed some light over this? Helen picks up the phone. Logan answers.

- "Winter, Logan speaking."
- "Hi, Logan. Its Helen. May I speak to Renee please?"
- "I'm sorry Helen, she is not home at the moment. Garden club. Renee won't be home until later tonight. Is there anything I can help you with my dear?"
- "I'm not sure? Maybe?, What do you know about some old notebooks?"
- "Notebooks?"
- "I found them at the back of the corner kitchen cupboard."
- Logan, remained silent.
- "Logan?'"
- Helen continued. "interesting reading, they have names, amounts. And range over 12 years. From '1975' up until

'1991'. There's records and receipts for builders, suppliers and bank loans?..... Anything yet...... Mr Winter?" Asked Helen.

- "Nope! Sorry dear. Doesn't ring any bells. Could they be Craig's?"
- "I doubt it, Mr Winter. Craig keeps his papers at our office in Hillstem. These books were. Well, are here. Besides, the dates? Craig would of only been a baby."
- Logan, still silent. Suddenly spoke. "Dear, you said '75'-'91'? is that correct?"
- "Yes, that's right."
- "It's coming to me. I remember know. Those notebooks would be the account records from the time Renee and I ran 'Country Life' our Bed and breakfast accommodation at 'Winter Forth'.

"Soon after I met Renee. She confided in me, her dream of someday having enough land where she could run a bed and breakfast. Much of the cooking was done by Renee herself. Home-made pies both sweet and savoury, cookies, cakes and quiche. "Eventually we hired a chef. And to accommodate those guests who wished to cook or prepare their own food. Both buildings had access to a communal kitchen. "They also shared an entertainment area, a laundry and communal garden. Renee's wish 'that there be a place where city people could experience life in the country.' "Hence the 'Country Life' bed and breakfast in Hillstem." Said Logan.

- Helen, now amazed. Excitedly said. "country Life' the bed and breakfast? I knew it was in Hillstem. But that's located here! Wow! I had heard about this growing up in Runegate. "Many of my friends and neighbours came out here with their families, during the school holidays. Helen then said. "That would be why amongst those books. Was a scrapbook, full of guest comments and pictures."

- Logan remarked, "Ah, school holidays. Our busiest and most popular times. Visitors mailed pictures back to us. "Kids in their overalls, sons/daughters in the milking sheds, their children splatted with mud whilst feeding the pigs. "Families standing by newly planted vegies."

- "How come Craig never told me about this? Come to think of it you and Renee never told me about this either! What happen? "Why do records stop at the end of '91'?"

"We had two growing teenage boys to look after. Boys who wanted to go away camping, fishing and have family trips together. "I realize now, that we could have hired people to run it for us, whilst we were away. Mrs Sherwood was secretary/receptionist. "But Renee, was always so passionate about this venture. She felt it more personal greeting and interacting with the guests herself. And I along with Marcus got to speak with many a traveller about their horses."

- "Hold up! This manor we live in. Would not accommodate the amount of guests and facilities that these books clearly identify! "Were the houses demolished? Removed as a whole? Did you sell the land they were on? "Because looking around here now. I can't see anything. "And no one would want to sleep above the horses in a stable. Just for a country experience. Trust me!"

- Logan, [laughed] "No, my dear. That's pretty funny though. Its located down the back end of the estate."

- Helen, [confused] said, "the back? she paused. Then continued. I've seen down the back. there are two crop fields, one tall silo, the windmill, a row of tall oak trees. "Similar to the ones that run along both sides of our driveway.[only taller] Behind those oak trees, is just bush land! Right?"

- "No, there is a track, behind those trees. "Cutting through and along the bushy area. It winds around to 'Country life'."
- Helen exclaimed, Wow! I believed beyond the fields. That land is owned by the people behind us.

Logan then said, "We have neighbours to both our left and right. 'Winter Forth' is a 55 acre estate. The area, down the back was originally cleared when my dad Charlie, kept his cows there. "Picture this Helen, if you would? Our mailbox is at the top of our driveway. Then you come to the turning circle. "The longest part of our visible land is the billabong. "We never counted, the 55 acres in width. We measured by length! "We only ever lived on about 15-25 acres. Hence..... the space down the back...... voila, 'Country Life'."

"That is so cool Logan. Thank you for sharing this with me. Your tale has inspired me. "When Craig gets home, im gonna ask him to tell me more. "And if he is interested. We'll speak on a re-establishment. "Please do say hello to Renee for me, when you see her. We'll be in touch with you soon. "You and Renee, would no doubt like to join us. When/if we re visit 'Country Life'?"

- "We would love that dear. I'll inform Renee. All I'll say to her is 'The dream lives on!' She'll be so enthusiastic. "Also... Renee is the only one who knows where to locate the keys and the permits."
- "Good bye Helen."

[Craig just got home] Helen said. "When you're ready. Can you please join me in the lounge/family room? "I'd like to speak with you." Craig sits down, Helen sits in the reclining armchair next to him. Helen begins.

- "Craig, what comes to your mind. When I say 'Country Life'?"
- 'Country life'?, Wow! I've not heard that name since -"
- Helen, interrupts and says "1991?"
- "Ok, that's eerie, honey. How did you do that? "I was just gonna say about 1991. [sniffs] mmm, is that a roast beef I smell? "Where is Mrs Sherwood? I missed saying hi to her when I arrived."
- "I made it. I gave her the night off. And Lucy is staying with my parents."
- "Ooh, so you're saying were all alone? Hmm? He gives Helen a suggestive hug."

"No! but I appreciate the thought. [they kiss] she sits back down and says. "I also invited Russell and Cherry to join us. "Who should be arriving shortly. As I was saying, 'Country Life.' In my hunt through the kitchen for a roast recipe. "I came across some old notebooks. Unsure what they were? I called looking for your mum, hoping she'd know? "Instead I got your father, so I asked him. if he knew what these books are? Wow, he knew. We had a long talk. "He told me all about the dream your mother had of opening a bed and breakfast. Here at 'Winter Forth'. "And according to these notebooks [fans them out and points to them] plus the talk with your dad. "That is exactly what they did here for a time!"

- Craig sighed, 'Country Life' "I was only young. But I recall it fondly. "The treats that mum made. Carrots we ate, straight from the garden. "Mum even made her own bread. So soft and sooo —"
- Helen interrupted. "Craig!"
- "Why are you snapping at me? I was only a kid!"
- "Is that all you have to say?"

"alright, I'll tell you. Just give me a moment. Craig closed his eyes. Then continued. Right, ah yes. "I remember one building was called 'Proudly pure' and the other one was called 'Friendly Farm' they each had two family room apartments and two double room apartments. "From the lobby you could walk down either buildings hallway. "In the 'Proudly Pure building' there was one room. "Which was only used if a single person or travelling business man was just stopping through."

- "Craig, I want to speak with you about re opening it to the public once again. "Maybe we can hold an anniversary. Invite some of the past guests to visit again and share their experiences?"
- "That would be great. What did dad say about this?"
- "He seemed eager. Told me he was going to speak with your mum. "Apparently she is the only one who knows where the keys and permits ended up?"
- "This is exciting, as soon as we hear from my mum and dad. We'll venture down the back."
- Helen, looked sternly at Craig. Then she said, "down the back!" As simply as that, huh? "Of course you can say it so casually. You knew about it all the time!," Helen shook her head, looked down and sighed. She then looked up and said "There is just one more thing I need from you, Mr Craig Daniel Winter!"
- Craig said, "oh!" And leaned in to give her a passionate kiss.
- "Helen stepped back. "No! An apology. You should have told me about this!"
- "But it was.......', No one has even stayed ...."
- "Uh! Excuses...."
- 'You're right, darling. I'm sorry for not telling you about this, Craig asked. Can you ever forgive me?"

- [Knock, knock.]
- "That'll be Russell and Cherry. Come here, Mr Winter. Helen kisses him, gives him a hug and sweetly says "I already have, you get the door please. I'll be in the kitchen."

12th September 2000

It's been almost three years now since Helen and Craig were married and spent their honeymoon in New York, a bit of a working holiday. Although it was another destination Helen had her heart set on. Craig knew of a location, where he could attend a convention and visit with a new contractor regarding future timber and building supplies. They were there for two weeks. There was much Helen still wished to see. But she couldn't wait to return to 'Winter Forth Farm.' There's just something to be said. Of that all too comforting feeling of snuggling up in your own bed. Trains go by regularly there. For them, their sounds have never been an imposition. If anything a comfort. They both love the atmosphere at 'Winter Forth.' This farm has been in Craig's family for four generations, passed down to the eldest son. So it goes without saying that when Craig and Helen have a son. It will one day belong to him. Lucy is now 2 years old and loves spending time outside with her Border collie puppy M&M. [Messy Meg] this nick name originated from Lucy's many attempts to pronounce her full name. But all that could be deciphered was "mmmeem." Therefore it just stuck. Lucy and M&M are the best of friends even with her father's disapproval of the times she spends inside with her. And mum complaining about the hair and fleas everywhere. Lucy particularly enjoyed having her beside her during bad weather. It has been attempted to leave her outside at night. But M&M would sob, at times it sounded louder than the passing trains at the top of the driveway. When we would go to town or visit grandparents. The only thing that soothed her was the sound of our vehicle returning home. M&M leaped through the pet door and eagerly jumped into Lucy's arms. Goodness help us, when Lucy begins kindergarten. Hopefully then M&M will be comforted by the sound of the bus pulling up at the top of the driveway. When we re tell our Paris story, to family and friends. They always ask. "what does that portrait display?" they even speculate as to what was chosen?

The funniest ones we've heard. Are "Craig is a hunter, and you're a 1950's house wife." Or "you two represented a famous actress and actor!" Craig just chuckles at them in response. Even my parents, lovingly greet Craig. Hug him and ask "What's in that photo of you and Helen from Paris?" He just [chuckles] to himself, looks over at me then leaves the room. The closest anyone has ever come to a reveal was the day Craig answered.

- "I made the final choice. We were going to be...... only there was this lovely couple on their honeymoon from Davenport, Tasmania. "Turns out they chose this destination especially to visit 'Old Tramway' wishing to recreate their engagement picture. "Which was taken two years earlier. Suffice was to say, they ended up with....... "So we decided to go with Helen's second choice, incorporating my secret suggestion." It still remains a mystery. With the truth spoken only between them.

Chapter Eleven

Malcolm Scott Winter's story

Craig stood up from the kitchen table, bought his plate over to the bench then placed his arms around Helen's waist and said 'thanks Honey that was delicious.' He then wandered out onto the front veranda which adjoins the side kitchen door. He looked out around the grounds, with it being spring the grass is a beautiful shade of green[sniffs] ah! There's nothing like that fresh cut grass smell. Craig then sat down on the wicker sofa. Russell and Wilson came out to join him, sitting in the two nearby armchairs. Russell handed Craig a cup of coffee.

- Craig took a sip then placed his cup down on the table. He looked toward Wilson, then looked at Russel and asked them. "Hey do you guys remember awhile back on this very veranda, Grandma Marian came to visit? A long conversation to-"
- Wilson [interrupted] "conversation? Heh! That implies speaking together, people conversing with one another. "As I recall it Grandma Marian, did all the talking. Telling us a story, a very looong story."
- "Oh yeah!, I remember we sat here. "Much like we are now and Grandma Marian sat by the lounge room window in her rocking chair." replied Russell.

- Wilson said. "That's right, she told us of our great, great, grandfather Malcolm Scott Winter and how he had acquired 'Winter Forth Estate.'
- "Estate!? Questioned Russell. But this is a-"
- "Yes. I know, a farm. replied Craig. "Actually for a brief period. My grandfather, Charlie ran it as a cattle ranch. I guess prior to that it was just an estate."
- Russell added "I remember that afternoon well. "Grandma Marian, had stayed here about a week. "And that was the day before she was due to return home."
- "Ooh yes, she was baking her specialty, apple pie." Which was always served with your choice of home-made custard or freshly whipped cream." Said Wilson then he continued. "Most of us were out here on this veranda, waiting for it to be ready. Come to think of it. "Due to the stories length, Its amazing the pie wasn't burnt."
- Craig replied "No, no. Bro. Grandma stopped speaking when it was ready. "Don't you remember that? She may have spoken longer if not for our oven timer.

Craig [sipped his coffee] then asked "Do either of you guys, happen to recall how that story went?"

- A puzzled Russell, scratched his head.
- Wilson shifted uncomfortably in his chair.

Craig waited a moment, looked at them both again. "No, huh? Well... you two are in luck. Because I do." Grandma Marian nestled back gently into her rocking chair [she sighed] then began. [Craig narrating story] "Back in the 1900's, well to be precise 1902. Malcolm Winter was an active member with the local council. An proposal was just granted for the commencement of laying the rail road and building Kanelake, rail way station. When the day come to start breaking ground. Malcolm put in a lot of extra hours. [Clears his throat] and continues, "you see that guest cottage over there, halfway between the turning circle and the top of the driveway. Craig points it out. That's where Malcolm lived during that time. Getting to work daily was nice and handy for him. He had the use a company vehicle for when he had to pick up tools or small supplies. All this area out the front from here[base of the steps- east of driveway] this was all owned by the council. The proposed layout for the railway station, required 35-40 acres of clearing. However those plans only allowed freight trains for carrying wheat, grain and coal only. Which meant that those lines couldn't safely or more importantly legally accommodate passengers or commercial transits. For this the council would require an additional 40acres of land. A meeting was arranged, with an open discussion as to how? And where? The extra acreage would be acquired from? Malcolm's cottage was on the 10 acres that he owned with a clear accessible boundary. Being Malcolm was their most avid worker during this project. He personally petitioned the council with a request in acquiring the additional land needed. [pointing out the long boundary to the left] the day the approval came back, Malcolm was over the moon. Only when the work got completed. It was discovered that by some error or department mix up. 75 acres in total had been cleared instead of the approved 40 acres. The council now realized they have ample foundations to secure three railway lines, one freight line and two commercial lines. And the railway station. No one came forward in defence of the error. Therefore It was agreed within the assigned committee, that Malcolm would be offered the additional 35 acres. At a fraction of the normal listing price, of course. Malcolm accepted, adding a counter offer. He said "I live across the road. Could I be granted an additional 35 acres next to my existing 10 acres? I'm happy to purchase the land required for this railway project and donate it to the community of Kanelake. You see where I have my 10 acres. My father Scott. Worked and lived all his life not far from here. Farming is in my blood, so I moved to Hillstem from Sandgate, 3 hours west of here. With the hope of one day beginning my own generation farm. Raise crops, and a family.

The committee granted his request and Malcolm did as promised. He donated the land to the community of Kanelake. Kanelake was the next rural community from 'Winter Forth' before arriving into Hillstem. They built a storage warehouse and erected two grain silos. Which can be seen from the top of our driveway. [Quoting as Marian] "Which is why my dears. Today 'Winter Forth' is a 55 acre estate." The circular garden, out front there. [points] I believe you would call it 'a turning circle' it began when the driveway got cleared. A lot of dirt and rocks got dumped there. Down the back of the manor. Just before the wheat field, there's a narrow brook, if I recall correctly -?

-   Yes, that's right. There's also a dirt path running alongside it. Said Wilson

Craig continues as Marian. "That brook, wasn't there naturally, Malcolm dug it himself with just two tools. Determination and a shovel. He discovered a natural spring. Malcolm placed the boulder in front of it. The water now flows up then runs down over the boulder.

Your great, great grandfather Malcolm, placed it there in symbolisation. That boulder was from the first breaking ground for the railway project. He then etched into it two W's. Winter and Wilkons. And chiselled some lines to appear as a waterfall, flowing into the brook. Mounted on the side of Malcolm's cottage is a plaque honouring him. "You've probably all read this! But I'll tell you anyway, it reads '7th November 1902, in dedication to Malcolm Scott Winter, for his tireless efforts establishing the new railway station.' Dedicated by Honourable Councillor Hugo Whitman, department of city planning. Hillstem, 1902. Whilst working on this project for the council Malcolm met and fell in love with Isabelle Wilkons. She was the youngest daughter of Bruce Wilkons. The lead graphic designer, assigned to the project. They married on the 16th of June 1903 right here at 'Winter Forth' and together bought an additional 10 acres. So thus we have 10, Malcolm owned, 35 he was 'gifted' and 10 investment = 55acres. They went on to have two beautiful children together. A son —

- Russell suddenly stood up, and asked. "What was that moaning sound she made?"
- "yeah, that was weird to me too," agreed Craig.
- "Grandma, was obviously thinking about grandpa Charlie," added Wilson.

They also had a daughter, named Hilary. It hurt Malcolm and the children deeply, losing Isabelle on the 3rd of August 1950. Then, sadly Malcolm passed away on the 20th of October, that same year. Charlie, being the eldest boy had 'Winter Forth' left to him. Hilary grew up here, then moved to Victoria. When she was 18. She studied hard for near two years and became manager at a real estate agency. Hilary, snatched up the opportunity to oversee a country estate restoration. A dashing young expert, Paul. Was assigned to her from another branch —

- Wilson [interrupted] "Hang on, are you speaking of uncle Paul?"
- "yes, Craig answered. Then continued. "Where was I?, Ah, yes. They dated for 6 months. It took a further 6 months, before Hilary told her parents. She had actually fallen in love with Paul Hill."

Charlie, remained here at 'Winter Forth' working for the council as his father had done. It was through this occupation he met a lovely woman, named Marian Huston.

- Both Russell and Wilson said in unison. "This is when we saw that wide, proud smile upon her face. She was talking about herself. They giggle. Please go on Craig"

Marian, was the local librarian. And lived in the city of Hillstem. They courted [that's 'dated' for you young folk.] for 2 years then settled here at 'Winter Forth'. Together they had three children, two sons Logan and Timothy. And a daughter, they named Susan. They all grew up here. Timothy went on to live in Ashhern, when he was 21. Your father, Logan got a letter from him recently. He's eagerly awaiting the fishing season to begin. At 22, Susan moved to Tempurst and became a teacher. Logan, remained here. My son Logan, has not shared with me the how and why? But he has remarked to me on more than one occasion. "That being here, has been one of the best things that ever happened to him. In fact he –"

- [beep, beep, beep.] remarked Russell.
- Craig stopped. Looked over to Russell and said "I believe this is just when you interrupted her. Saying "that was the oven timer" you sniffed deeply, then said 'Mmm that pie, really does smell amazing Marian. Can we go check on it?'
- Wilson added, "that's when Grandma, herself took a whiff."
- And replied "Yes I believe, it is done!" She stood up and asked us. "Okay who would like cream? And who would like custard?"
- Craig [laughed]
- What's so funny?" asked Russell and Wilson.
- We all replied in unison "Me!"
- Then grandma Marian called us all inside.

Chapter Twelve

⚜

Welcome Jamie

On the 18th of December 2000 at 3.20am Helen and Craig welcomed a beautiful baby boy Jamie Robert Winter. HCC 54cms, 52cms long, weighing 2700kgs. He has his grandad's chin and his parents brown hair. That afternoon saw many visitors drop by the hospital. Including grandad Logan, Grandma Renee, Uncle Wilson and Aunty Monique. All keen to welcome this beautiful new generation. Helen's Sister Mary was at Winter Forth, looking after big sister Lucy.

19th of September 2002.

Lucy's teacher, Miss Farrell announced today. "We will have a pet show and parade next Thursday the 26th." Soon after Lucy got home, her mum Helen found the notice in her bag. And spoke to her about it.

- "Lucy, this sounds like a fun day, a pet parade."
- Lucy announced, excitedly. "Yep, me and Shearer, will have a good day."
- Craig and Helen, adamantly replied. "Were sorry, my dear. 'Shearer' is too big. We think it'll be best sweetie, if you bring M&M instead. We'll drive you to school. Stay for the

parade and M&M can return with us. You'll get the school bus home."

[Lucy's pet parade] M&M hung her head out the window the whole trip, School was only a 45 min drive. Within the school grounds of course. M&M needed to be kept on her leash.

- Miss Farrell, called out "everyone please line up along the path outside. "I'll call each of you by your last name. "Collect your pet or toy from your parent/caregiver. Parade your pet around this circle, say your name, age, say your pet or toys name. Their age and why you chose that name?"
- Julie Walters, just had her turn. Lucy stood up proudly, walked up to her parents, took the lead from her mum then walked toward the circle. Praising M&M along the way. "Good girl, well done." Than told her to "sit." M&M sat beside Lucy. Lucy, gave her a pat. Than began her presentation. "My name is Lucy Crystal Winter, I'm 4. This is my dog M&M. She is 2years old. Messy Meg, is her name. she loves to bring garbage into our kitchen. She's called M&M because I couldn't say her name at the time. [giggles]

19th December 2004, Jamie kindergarten.

Having just celebrated Jamie Winter's 4th birthday he will begin Kindergarten in January, 2005. Jamie's parents agreed that he too could have a pony. His father, Craig arranged to take him down the road, to 'McCarthy's Ranch' their neighbour. This is a visit Craig has looked forward to. Especially after seeing how happy Lucy was when she'd picked out 'Shearer' from the very same ranch. The afternoon has finally arrived. Jamie, could barely contain his excitement. Mr McCarthy was very pleased to welcome them. He had three ponies to choose from. Jamie, holding his father's hand walked over to the stables. On the left was an all-black pony. On the right, a white pony with four black spots. The pony in the middle. Was remarkable. He had a dark brown coat, a long black mane and tail with black boots, with some light to dark yellow spots along his back. 'Trifle!' Jamie called out excitedly and ran up to the pony in the middle. Mr McCarthy even offered to give him free riding lessons. To this Craig happily accepted. Helen recalls, one particular afternoon. She was out in the laundry room. She peeked through the window. And saw such an adorable sight. It was Jamie. Helen, looked at her watch and said aloud "yep, 4pm my little lad is on his way to the stable, wearing.... [Peers in a little closer, giggles] is that? It is. "One of Craig's old jackets, obviously way too big for him. "And that hat, its near covering his face it's soo big. "What are those on his feet? [laughs] a pair of Uncle Wilson's boots. "Oh my goodness, the poor dedicated lad. Craig did say, 'Trifle' would be his responsibility. "He is determined, and responsible. I'll give him that." In one hand he's holding the feed bucket. In the other hand, Jamie is holding his riding blanket. Jamie walked toward the bell. An ingenious idea, created by Logan. It hangs just above the stable door way. From a young age the horses were trained to assemble when they hear it ring three times. Jamie put his blanket on the hook and placed the bucket on the shelf. He then rang the bell three times [ding! Ding, ding.] then waits a bit for 'Trifle' to appear at the stable gate.

15th of December 2005 Jamie's surprise gift

Jamie will soon be turning 5 and he hasn't shared with anyone his birthday wish. Helen watches him eagerly, trying to guess? Waiting for a slip up in words, anything that might give her an idea to what he desires. Helen has made suggestions such as "if you could have 3 wishes, what would you wish for? Each time Helen got the same reply from Jamie

- "Mum, if I tell you, it won't come true!"

Only days to go and still not a clue. No one was aware if he'd spoken to anyone else? Then last night we received a call from Wilson. Craig took the call but didn't tell Helen any of what they'd talked about. Craig just put the phone down, grabbed his car keys and announced

- "I'm going to see Mr McCarthy."
- Puzzled, Helen thought to herself "at night. What could he need there?"

Jamie kept his same behaviour/routine each afternoon. First homework, chores, watch the trains rock on by for a bit. Then take a short ride on 'Trifle' either around the garden or along the billabong. Jamie has never shown any interest in competitive riding or show jumping. They have done small jumps. Though usually just for fun. Unlike his older sister Lucy, racing and jumping is all she dreams about. It's a shared interest between her and grandad Logan. Craig has just returned from Mr McCarthy's ranch. It didn't seem like he'd been gone for long time. He didn't take the trailer, so it wasn't to drop off anything. I can also eliminate a catch up. What's he up to then? Helen thought. However knowing Craig as she does, it was no doubt something mysterious, surprising. Helen headed out the back, looked over to the stable, the garage. Odd, no sign of Craig. He didn't walk past me, he's not near the car. That man of mine was and still is full of surprises! She began to head back inside, soothing that Craig is bound to turn up soon enough. Helen took the first step and began climbing the stairs back onto the front veranda. Then all of a sudden she was stopped. Something or someone tugged on her dress. She'd cried out "what was that!?" Turned and saw an excited Jamie. Jumping up and down. Then he asked

- "Mum, mum. Did you see it? Did, Dad tell you?"
- [Helen sighs] "Jamie, oh honey, settle down my boy. Now slowly, Have I seen what?"
- "My new saddle", Mr McCarthy gave me his son's old one. He lets me ride 'Falcon' and use this saddle. Now it's mine."

Craig's brother Wilson occasionally stays at Winter Forth, while Monique is away travelling for work. This has been a god send not only to Craig but Helen also. He helps preparing the kids for school, farm chores and Wilson hasn't objected to the occasional child minding. Craig and Helen, can then take the opportunity to go out to dinner with Helen's parents. Every which way you looked around the grounds of 'Winter Forth' there was so much scenery to enjoy. The flowers, the billabong, chickens running about freely. The occasional sheep throughout the paddock. Clear sunny days, Jamie enjoyed riding 'Trifle', taking in all that beauty. But on a cold, rainy days. He was found to be doing indoor activities, up in his room. One heavily raining day Helen and Craig happened to walk by Jamie's room. They peeked in the ajar door and remarked to each other.

- "look at our boy, Craig. His building with his blocks. Graphic paper and pen on his corner desk. You know, "I believe he'll become a builder or graphic designer one day."
- "I don't know. That hand eye coordination when he plays those computer games. "That's my deep thinking boy right there. I'd bet, an architect or perhaps an accountant. "Maths is one of his favourite subjects at school –"
- "Ah! No dear, he is good at math... It's not a favourite subject!"
- "You're right of course, my love."
- Helen smiles, "I never tire from hearing that."

Chapter Thirteen

3rd of January 2007, Rural Women's Association Meeting

H elen is an active member of the local RWA, Rural Women's Association with 12 financial Members. Including Meredith Sherwood and Renee winter. Grandma Marian is a charter member. Meetings are held on the 1st & 3rd Wednesday of each month for two hours in Sagehurst. Helen joined a month after moving to 'Winter Forth' at first for a social activity. Living her whole life in a city, Helen believed it to be a great opportunity. As it would acclimatize her transition to country life. Then she began getting to know her fellow members. Much of who lived nearby and within the community. The meeting venue is an hour's drive for Helen. Two other ladies meet her at 'Winter Forth' they have a cuppa together then all travel over in one car. At her third meeting Helen become a member and took on the PRM, public relations manager. Their meeting were usually related to food drives, clothing, markets, charitable donations or community cent auctions. By the end of last year, RWA had gained four new members. Unfortunately two of them weren't able to renew their memberships. During tonight's meeting Helen, announced. "As your PRM, I'd like us to have a vote. Where we can implement these new promotional themes. It's my wish, that going forward. They inform, encourage and generate more interest in our club. As well as make our local communities aware of the type of support and assistance we provide. I was finalizing this over the weekend with VPM, Mrs Sherwood. Everyone remembers fellow member, Meredith Sherwood. Who by the way sends her apologies for tonight, her husband Marcus is feeling unwell."

Themes we come up with are (1) pot luck dinner (2) date night (3) we share, we care (4) gather around and (5) merry me. I've printed up more detailed descriptions about each one on these pamphlets, available here in the middle of the table. Feel free to take one.

1) Pot luck dinner: meeting place will be at a different member's house in rotation, where everyone brings a dish to share.
2) Date night: held at our local RSL where each member brings there partner/significant other.
3) We share, we care: people from the community bring in unwanted/unused or pre loved items. We then re-distribute them to neighbouring crisis support centres, halfway houses, churches, schools etc;
4) Gather around: an invitation gets sent to other RWA groups for a combined meeting.
5) Merry me: a wine and cheese tasting event with information handouts (member drive) Highlighting member achievements/accomplishments, past success stories. We even gather some local caterers and artists to showcase some of their creations.

Flyers will go out prior to the event, inviting the general public to come along. Naturally we can't do all these each month. Helen suggested.

- "Alternating them would be best. It's not a guarantee, it will generate new members. But it will definitely be fun and most importantly everyone can be involved."
- Mrs Hewitt, our secretary. Gave everyone a ballad sheet, telling them "I'll collect them afterwards. No names, please. It's completely anonymous. Circle your preference/interest from most favourable to least favourable. When finished place your ballad face down in front of you on the table."
- Helen reminded, "Once Jessica, has collected all ballads. We'll break for a short supper. If during this time you should have any questions, please approach myself or Jessica [Mrs Hewitt] and we'll happily answer them for you."
- 5 mins later. "Ladies, lets resume. Please take your seats everyone. We'll begin with general business then read out the voting results," assured Helen.
- "Mrs Hurst, will you please take the minutes whilst Mrs Hewitt is busy?" Mrs Hurst agrees.
- 20 mins later. "Thank you, Mrs Hurst, and thank you all for your participation. The results are in. I'd like to invite Secretary Jessica to join me up the front.
- "Thanks Helen. We have 2 for pot luck dinner, 3 for merry me, 2 for gather around, 2 for we share, we care and 3 for date night. A tie, Mrs Winter. 'Hmm, well im no politician but I suggest alphabetically? Does this suit everyone?"
- Everyone agreed, "Carried" said Helen. She continues, "Excellent, I thank you all again for your cooperation. Date night will be first. And next we'll arrange 'Merry me. We have around 15 minutes remaining of tonight's meeting. How about we work on setting a date and designing an invitation.
- [10 mins later] Mrs Hewitt announced, "Date night will be on the 24th of January. At the Hillstem RSL Club, 6:30 - 10pm. Which is about three weeks away."

- Treasurer, Mrs Lorraine Myers said. "I'll confirm the booking with the RSL."
- Jessica added. "I will arrange for this draft flyer to be finished, copied and dispersed throughout town. Also I will be available should anyone require any assistance."

Monique has just returned home, for the last two weeks she was in Morocco. Monique was part of a committee, sent there to acquire fabric samples. Wilson is always pleased to see her home, he misses her so when she's away. As much as he really enjoys helping Craig and Helen around 'Winter Forth.' My guess is he doesn't miss all the chores, required by the farm. Probably, reminds him of when he grew up there. I honestly believe he's happy spending quality time with he's Niece and Nephew. But longs to be back home also. The next few days after Monique returns. She always shares such fascinating travel stories. Tells us of music she's heard. Places she saw and even some people she saw. Although working with celebrities. I'll bet she isn't allowed to speak of 'special clients.' She works directly with. Helen giggles,

- "I remember once in our kitchen, Monique told me of her time in London during the Christmas holidays. To this day, she won't share all the details. Also we are not allowed to ask anymore. One particular afternoon in the airport terminal. In her own words 'suffice was to say, A certain underwear model. Was without her.. underwear!'
- [giggling] Monique then stood up and walked out of the kitchen. On her way, I know she quietly said to herself 'What some people will try?'
- When Monique and Helen have spoken in the past. Helen tries saying. "My goodness you would think......? "Would know better huh? "Each time, Helen throws in a different name of a well-known model, male and female alike.

"Monique neither confirms nor denies them. She just wonders off giggling again. "Damn, she just won't give in."
- Craig said. "It's been rumoured that Wilson knows. Yet he remains neutral, shaking his head. As if to sternly imply, 'don't ask me!'

Wilson Is the youngest son of Logan and Renee Winter and like his nephew Jamie has always loved building blocks. Hopes were expressed that one day he too would become a carpenter. Nope, Wilson surprised everyone when he became a painter. Also he enrolled in an online course, studying to become an architect. Monique and Wilson don't yet have children of their own. So their three bedroom home in Sagehurst, really does seem big for just the two of them. Their hopeful for children, just not as yet. They're both focused on work and enjoying each other's company. It's been a year since they eloped in New Zealand. Monique needed to be there for two to three weeks for work. Instead of missing one another. Wilson excitedly announced "I'll go with you." They were engaged. At the time. Monique didn't know, Wilson already had a plan. To marry her whilst there. Monique, has some annual leave saved up. Wilson, works for himself. He can get things done as long as there is desk space available. Knowing they'll both have the time and freedom, Wilson booked has already booked a Caribbean cruise for their honeymoon. They'll leave around a month after they get back from New Zealand.

Chapter Fourteen

---❦---

Date night

Helen regularly goes to the shopping centre. And she understands that it gets very busy at times. But this day the 24th of January, was ridiculous. Not a hair appointment to be had, you couldn't move around in any of the clothing stores or shoe shops.

- Helen said to herself "Girl, if you don't already have a nice pair of shoes! Then an old pair will just have to do!"

All the women were buzzing around. Fixing their hair, nails and waxing galore. All in excitement of tonight. Helen peeked in at most of the shops/salons. She didn't just see women in there. Some men were in front of the mirrors too, getting shirts or shoes. Having a haircut and or a shave. I'm not 100% certain, but am positive they were a part of the um waxing process too. Helen thought, It's 1pm now. I'll make an appointment and come back later. she wasn't thrilled, when the only time available was at 4.30.

- Helen said "That won't work." She knew, she had to be at the Leagues club by 6pm. Helen told the lady, "I have an important date tonight. Is there anything earlier available?"

The lady looked again. She then went and asked someone else. Someone who, I assume was either her assistant or the actual hair dresser. Then she returned, and said.

- "Ok the earliest I can do is 2pm."
- "I'll take it", Helen said happily.

The centre hadn't been this busy since two days before Christmas. Helen decided to head back home, Monique and Wilson are coming over to join us for date night. Lucy and Jamie are staying with my parents, Grandma Becky and Grandpa Jerry. Helen and Craig, don't usually make the time to go out to dinner alone. Helen is pleased, Craig will be beside her. Tonight is not an official RWA meeting [was declared to postpone regular meet until next month] Helen, however still had a role to perform as coordinator. Whilst Craig was dressing for tonight he noticed, Helen left her wrap in the cupboard. He went downstairs, placed it around her shoulders and said. "here you are my dear" He then headed out to the car, waved out to his mother in law Becky then sat in the passenger side. Helen drove, Craig settled back into his seat. He closed his eyes and was suddenly reminded of another trip he made in the passenger's seat. It was when his Mother Renee, drove him into preschool in Sagehurst. Craig was especially excited as that day was Russell's 7th birthday.

[Craig reflecting back] Russell, my mate, my bro, and now business partner. Gosh, many years of sleepovers, camping and fishing trips, riding horses on the weekends, dirt bike riding at 'Rear Tyre'. Christmas holidays together. Russell turns 7 today, I was 6. I usually made friends quite easily. I mean, many 6 year olds are friends with everyone. None that compare to Russell Thompson. Craig continued. Now most kids will do anything to avoid going to school. But me, I loved going. I remember being very excited that day.

- Craig called out to his mum from the car "Mum, mum. I'm ready. We gotta go!"
- "Ok, give me a minute Craig!"

As soon as the car pulled up Craig come up to her door begging for Russell's gift which they picked out and wrapped over the weekend.

- "Hold on boy. We'll walk in together." Renee grabbed her bag and went to lock the car.
- "Mum the gift!," demanded Craig.
- "Here you go, handing Craig the gift and off he went.

There were two prep classes PB (Miss Bennett) and PR (Mrs Ryley) laughing, giggling to himself Craig ran over to Russell, calling out "bye mum!" On the way. He was glad to be in the same class as Russell. Craig, couldn't help but to recall. Just how many times Russell's mum had remarked 'you two are as close as brothers!' I remember some weekends where I wasn't able to stay over. If I or he hadn't done our chores, homework or if we had been misbehaving. Ah Russell, my mate, my brother, my bunk mate at University and now my business partner. They were such good times. We even -

- "Craig!" Helen interrupted Craig sat up "Here we are the leagues Club." Helen said.
- "Oh right, sorry hon. I was a million miles away thinking about Russell. It's a shame he and Cherry couldn't join us tonight. You look really beautiful tonight dear."
- "Thank you Hon, shall we go in?"
- [reception] "Good evening, I'm Helen Winter. We have a booking tonight, RWA party."
- "This is Garth, he'll take you to our function room."

During dinner, Mrs Hewitt handed out the flyers regarding the next event "Merry me' to be held on the 16th of March 2007. Then 'gather around' will be next month. Beginning at our venue then alternating to surrounding clubs. Then we'll alternate to surrounding clubs.

Chapter Fifteen

---❦---

18th of March 2007, Renee & Logan wedding anniversary

Helen and Craig are throwing an anniversary party at 'Winter Forth' For Renee and Logan, they've invited all their closest friends, family and some past guests to celebrate their 37th wedding anniversary. On the 16th of March 1970, he married his high school sweetheart Renee Parkes. Everyone who could be there turned up 'Winter Forth' was busting at the seams. It usually is busy but whoa! Thank goodness they have 55 acres. Some people called upon Logan to give a speech he just waved his hand and replied "Nah, she be right!" Applause got louder, then clapping eventually got quicker. When Logan heard everyone's insistence. He put his hand in the air, raised up his glass, leant down slightly and clinked his wife's glass. Crowd ceased and quieted back down, some seats were dispersed throughout. Now standing at the front of the crowd. Logan begun.

- "My dear, I must toast you. You are a wonderfully strong woman not only tolerating me for more than 20 minutes, per day. "You've faithfully been by my side and put up with me for 20+ years. "I'm sure at times it hasn't been easy.

I've got mates, [smiled, looks around] who could tell you some stories.

- [STORIES, HUH! FACTS!] Someone calls out from the back.
- Logan just [chuckled] welcome to those friends, family and past guests who have gathered here today. "You've always been there for us, tilts his glass toward the back of the tent. "Then adds a cheeky grin. As if to say, you know who you are [chuckles]. Logan continued, "Renee and I thank our sons Craig and Wilson, and their wives Monique and Helen for organising all this and surprising us."
- Renee then added. "We believed we were being called to babysit tonight. I said to Logan. "Tell them we have plans. Thinking on it now. I'm happy he convinced me to go."
- "It's great seeing you all. [laughs] Thank you again everyone for coming, hope you have a great night." He then leant down kissed Renee and whispered "I love you sweetness. Will you honour me with this dance Mrs Winter?"
- Renee took her husband's arm just as the band started playing 'save the last dance for me'. "Yes, Mr Winter, and they stepped onto the wooden dance square. "She then said to Logan. "We haven't danced together, since our silver anniversary, 12 years ago."

Later that evening Craig was clearing away some of the empty glasses from the outdoor table. When his father walked up beside him, threw his arms around him and said "Thank you so much Craig for doing this. "Would you like me to lend a hand packing things away?" "Nah, Dad we've got this you're good." Replied Craig. Logan then sat down on a deck chair by the billabong [sighed] took another sip from his beer, looked out over the garden. Admired the hedges planted along the edge of the water.

Chapter Sixteen

❦

Meeting Renee

Logan closed his eyes and within minutes found his mind starting to wander back in time. He saw the day he and Renee, had made those flower beds and planted the small hedges. He shut his eyes again. Now, Logan sees the house in Sagehurst. He lived there, for a year. Because his mother Marian. Secured a job as the local librarian. The year was 1961, January 10th 1961 to be exact. Logan was beginning year 9 at Sagehurst High School [Giggling] he then let out a contented [sigh] Logan thought to himself. The first day of school is an awkward at best. But for me, it was even worse. He was the new student... the new student who had an 'accident', a silly one. Logan wished he could just forget it all together. But to deny it had occurred. Would rob him of a much more pleasant and meaningful memory. Because the day of this shameful memory was also the day he met Renee Parkes. It was a lovely summer morning in QLD, beautiful not as hot as its been of late. He seemed to breeze through all his morning subjects. Then came the afternoon. A beautiful young lady met his gaze in the hallway, he remembers as clear as if it were yesterday. They both went to enter the classroom for history, second last subject for the day. In the room there were only two vacant desks. The young lady took the one in the back corner and Logan went toward the desk, right in front of her. Being a little nervous, he failed to look around. He quickly pulled his chair out to sit down. Only when he shifted his feet he didn't realise he was standing on two of these lovely ladies fingers. Logan didn't see, Renee was already knelt down beside her chair. Trying to retrieve the contents of her pencil case. When Renee sat down and attempted to open it up. It jammed, once it finally moved. Pens, pencils, erasers shook out. Hitting the floor, then starting to roll. Logan stepped back and immediately began apologising "sorry, I'm so sorry." While helping to rescue these items, they very nearly bumped heads on their way back up. "I guess I wasn't looking, here are your pencils." "Thanks" said Renee. They each took their seats. Logan learnt, including history they share three classes together every day. It's true, history has shown most young boys, often chase all the attractive girls. But when it came to Renee Parkes. Logan felt as if 'she was no ordinary attractive girl.' He found he was instantly smitten with her. Usually the knuckle down, concentrate on learning student. His mother, Marian was surprised to see Logan so unfocused. Chores rarely done, no interest in riding his horse. An 'I'll get to it' attitude regarding homework. [It was, February 1st 1961] Sagehurst high has their annual school fete on Saturday, 11th of February, It's a big event. Today is Wednesday, just 9 days away. Logan wished to ask Renee to go with him. But with each hypothetical scenario he created, he lost his nerve then his voice. The next morning, shortly after from class. I was standing by the port rack. Renee walked straight over to me. Noticing her strut/ pace. I began fretting. Darn, did her favourite sharpener roll too far away? Or did I damage her fingers more than I thought? She then politely said 'morning' and asked me 'if I'd help her study, for our upcoming history assignment.' I agreed. I was over the moon. Renee will be at my house this afternoon, studying for at least an hour. Surely I can produce the words to ask her then. 3.30, [knocks] Hi Renee, history right? Just through into here. I led her into the lounge room. I then asked would you.....? feeling, finally I have the words.

Um? Nothing... I changed to. Would you like to sit here or at the table? We proceeded with study. We laughed at stories she told me of her previous school. She told me of her dream of one day owning a large estate. I told her my embarrassing tale, all about the stool I hand made for my dad Charlie, last father's day. Logan [laughed] that chair is in my room. [giggles] I made it alright. Only to my proportions, not his. [they both laugh] Logan then continued. My dad, politely thanked me for the footstool. I declared 'it's a seat!' anyway, it made his day to present it to me. [what do you know, it fit.] The moment felt so perfect. Logan thought to himself. This is it, my chance. 4:20. I'll ask now. Logan turned to Renee and asked her, do you want to ....., [sighs] can I get you a drink? She smiled and said 'no thanks'. 4.30pm Renee, thanked me and went home. Tomorrow is Friday, I'll ask her then. [Ugh!] We have gym together. That won't go well. Then that arvo Renee will be away with her family. I may not get another opportunity. Definitely next week, I'll ask her then. Monday came and went. Tuesday came and went. Wednesday, [alright Logan, it needs to be today.] Just say it man! Hi, Renee right thru into here my Mum said we can use the sunroom, just before we start 'can I get you a drink? or Something to eat' asks Logan 'I'm fine, thank you' said Renee. She then asked me 'Where would you like to begin Logan? I believe, 'World war 2' had just been declared. We can cover the drafting process, if you wish?'

I replied, 'actually neither at the moment. I've really been hoping to ask, talk to you about something [cough, cough] [clears his throat] Renee, would you? Do you think?' staggered Logan. Renee looked at him [listening eagerly] Still a silent Logan, began again 'how about.....' Nothing. He's gone blank, silent again. Renee placed both her hands upon Logan's face and says 'yes, I would love to go to the fete with you.' Logan smiled, hardly believing what he'd just heard. [blushing] enthusiastically replies. 'I'll pick you up at 9:30am, we'll walk together.' Renee replied 'that won't be necessary, I'll meet you there. Hospitality, remember my dear. I'll already be there. Our class is making the cakes, slices and biscuits. However, I will be happy to walk home with you afterwards.' She gave him a hug and a kiss on the lips. Then said goodbye and went home. Logan thought wow! What a bumbling fool, I must have sounded like. In the end I didn't have to say a word. My Renee, really is such an amazing woman for knowing my mind like that. [smiles] (present) "Logan!" in the distance. Logan can hear Renee calling his name. he sat back up and walked back towards 'Winter Forth' Logan spotted Renee, standing near the back stairs. "What is it my dear?" asked Logan. "it's time we went home." [the next morning] Logan happily waltzed into his kitchen, kissed Renee on the lips, turned the jug on. And sat down. Smiling as he looked over at Renee. He said "what did I ever do, to deserve 37 years with you?" She walked over to him, hugged him and replied "exactly, what you're gonna do now. Make me a cuppa, when you have one." They laugh. [Ring, ring]

- "Winter, this is Renee Winter, hello?"
- "May I please speak with Mr Logan Winter?"
- "Yes, I'll put him on."
- "Logan, my darling. You're wanted on the phone."
- [Logan, having conversation] "Thank you, for your call. I'll be there shortly."

He hangs up the phone and sits down in their lounge room. Renee entered, sat beside him and asked,

- "who was on the phone, my darling?"
- "It was the hospital, Susan is there, with mum. My dad…., He… My father, Charlie has passed away. "He's care provider found him still in bed this morning. When she came to clean."

- "Oh my gosh, Logan. I'm so sorry to hear this," she places her arm around him. "Let's get dressed we'll head to the hospital."

2 hours later, Logan sat down with his father's Doctor. Who asked him, "when he last saw his father?"

- "Just last week. But I spoke with him, two days ago. He was meant to come to our anniversary party. Only he couldn't... because he...... gosh... he said he was feeling unwell. "Darn, I should have been with him. I thought it was nothing serious [cries a little]
- the doctor asked, "will you be alright Logan? Do you have someone with you?'
- "Yes my family is around the front."
- Ok says the doctor," he then continued. "Your father passed away early this morning. Peacefully in his sleep."
- Logan asked, "do we know how?"
- "It was just old age, Logan."

We all went back to 'Winter Forth. Then mum came back to our place with us. For two nights. Then she returned to her home. Having lost her beloved Charlie. Marian, fell into a depressive state. Not given up. Though gossipers believed, that was the case. Popular opinion became, she should 'go to a retirement village now.' Marian knew people meant well. But like any effective protester or strong woman. Marian stood firm always. Proudly saying to all. "I'd rather remain independent!" within 2 months, Marian and Logan, sold the house her and Charlie had in Hillstem. Marian moved in with her daughter Susan. After living with Susan ten months. Marian, sadly passed away peacefully. Also from old age, she was the same age as Charlie, 92 years young. R.I.P. Marian, Annabelle Winter nee [Huston} 03 September 1917- 09 February 2008. Beloved wife of

Charlie Winter [deceased] dear mother to Logan, Timothy and Susan. Cherished Grandmother to Craig and Wilson. Great grandma to Lucy and Jamie.

At the time of her passing, Marian was still a charter member of the RWA Rural Women's Association, Hillstem. [though inactive] a faithful bingo follower, book club member and rotary support worker. She hadn't volunteered with 'Hills op' a local charity shop for near 5 years. Though she still dropped in to see them whenever she could. And maintained monthly donations. Marian was well respected throughout the community. Marian will be lovingly remembered by her whole family. May she rest in peace, by God's side.

Here are some heartfelt tributes from we received via mail.

Logan and Renee,
12/02/08

Were so sorry to hear of the passing of your mother, Marian. When I moved here 10 years ago alone. I didn't know anyone. I was struggling to make ends meet. [moving costs, seeking employment] At the general store, one day she paid the difference in my grocery bill and gave me a lift home. We often caught up and had lunch together after bingo on Wednesday's.

Yours in sympathy
Mildred Green

Logan Winter and family,
12/02/08

You don't know me but my name is Phillip Whitman [Councillor]my great granddad was Hugo Whitman. He made a dedication to your Great grandfather Malcolm in 1902. It is somewhat of a legendary tale in this office. I've seen

the duplicate copy of the plaque in our archives.
Perhaps one day in the future, I can honour you
with a personal visit, remembering both our
grandfathers. I simply wish to express my deepest
sympathy for your family's loss. If there is ever any
way I can help you? Please contact me.

Yours
Cnr Phillip Whitman
Hillstem, council and agriculture.
11-14 Angus Street, Hillstem, Qld
Phone: 1300 268 247
Mobile: 0428 569 243
Email: Hillstemcounag.com.au

Lucy and Jamie Winter,
12/02/08

My sincere condolences to you both and your families on the passing of your great grandma Marian. We at 'Hillstem Community Church' will be forever grateful for the continued dedication, support and contributions she and Her late Husband Charlie have given over the years. They will both be remembered fondly. All our prayers and blessings at this difficult time.

Worship and thanks
Brenda Wilkes
Church Coordinator
0428 468 246

P.S.

I also wish to convey the communities respects. They all had many positive and fond memories of when Marian was the Hillstem local librarian.

❤❤❤❤❤❤❤❤❤❤❤❤❤❤❤❤❤❤❤❤❤❤❤❤❤❤❤❤❤❤

One afternoon by the front garden. Helen was sitting on the bench reading, when she was approached by Craig. Who asked "May I have this seat?'"

- Helen, giggled and replied. "Just for a moment. "See, my husband is due home any minute now. "I feel It only fair to warn you, he tends to get mighty jealous."
- "Is that so?," [laughs] he sits down beside her. "Perhaps he knows too well, just what a wonderful, supportive and caring woman you are. "And is afraid of you being stolen away!"

Craig then said to Helen. "You know how, Nightly news, phone apps, neighbours and or newspapers can predict weather forecasts. "Someone who claims to know the area well. Can achieve this foresight also. "my mum had this friend who in 20 years never paid any mind to weathermen. "He'd simply look out his doorway. Then decide, jacket? or umbrella? Living in QLD, we have seen our fair share of inconvenient flooding, we've faced and survived our droughts. "Do you remember that summer. We lived two months, keeping that survival kit by our back door? We stayed prepared. If we needed to be evacuated due to blazing, windy bushfires all around. "Am thankful 'Winter Forth' has always remained safe. [Crosses fingers] well so far anyway. "Mr McCarthy, maintains his estate religiously. As do the 'Thompsons' The area directly across from us 'railway yard' is faithfully maintained by the Kanelake council."

Helen then said. "I'll never forget how scared I was for our animals, around January 2006. Weather predicted storms, high winds, heavy rain. Informing we may face flooding rain. 55 acres, oak trees along our driveway and down the back. "I knew if we needed to. We could get out. "I did pray that the wind or lightning didn't cause them to fall or break branches. Luckily there was only leaves blown around and onto the paths. Strong winds but nothing out of place."

- "Unless we count the time, Jamie's underwear blew up onto our veranda roof," Craig [giggles] "Our manor, fortunately is on a slight rise. From the top of our driveway you head down to Mr McCarthy's ranch to the left and down to Farmer Garth's on our right."
- I'll grant you, Craig. There have been tough times. Sad times, challenges. There have also been so many happy times, proud moments and amazing supportive friends, community. [Helen kisses Craig passionately]
- "True, my dear," replies Craig. "It's not facing challenging situations. It is how we rise up afterwards. "Being here, having you and our children beside us.
- I have definitely understood "That no matter what befalls us in our lives, when you have special friends and family near you, you can face any problem!"
- They both smile
- "You're absolutely right. That is one of the many reasons, I love you, and I'll always will."
- "I love you too Mrs Helen, Patricia Winter. Mr Winter, before dinner would you care to join me for a stroll along the billabong?"
- "I would love to." They stand up together, and walk hand in hand toward the billabong.

Chapter Seventeen

---✣---

5th of May 2008. [backstory] Mrs Meredith Sherwood

D INNER!, Mr Winter!, Lucy!, Jamie! Come to the table please, Mrs Sherwood called out. This is what we mainly hear from Meredith. Meredith is a very lovely woman. Being she is only 5ft tall, I assure you. No one will or ever has looked down on her. She was born on the 7th of July 1950 in Runegate, QLD. and lived there with her family. After achieving a diploma in hospitality, she moved out of her family home and commenced working here at 'Winter Forth Farm' when she was 28. Looking upon her now, you see short silvery hair. According to dad plus various photos [she usually took, not posed for] and to ask Meredith herself. 'It is hard to imagine now with these grey hairs. That I was once straight, brown hair.' Mum and Meredith often joke and reminisce together over coffee. [giggling, laughing] as they remember. How they used to wear their hair when it was long. Mum said to Meredith 'you know, I'll bet there'd be less grey now, if I hadn't dyed it as regularly as I had.' Meredith is now 56. She's has two sisters. One whose three years older [Louise] and one who is a year younger [Carmen.] Marcus is Meredith's husband, they met here at 'Winter Forth.' Marcus, originally was hired just as a stable hand, to tend to the horses and maintain the stable. Over time he become so much more than that. A very efficient employee. He was 29, he made supply runs to town, upkeep the grounds and gardens. Although Marcus has been here a similar amount of time as Meredith. It doesn't mean they were a couple for all that time. In fact they never used to get along, Guests often said things like ' those two really hate each other!' the best comment I've heard was 'I'll bet Mrs Sherwood, has threatened to serve Marcus up a plate of that same muck, she accuses him of bringing in on his boots.' [laughs] When they announced their engagement, people laughed, as if they're making a joke. Unfortunately Meredith and Marcus were unable to have children of their own. Though Meredith certainly was no stranger to having children around. For years she would baby sit Louise's and Carmen's children. When anyone asked her 'wouldn't you prefer your own children?' Meredith replied, 'not at all.

Me and Marcus can spoil this lot, then hand them back to their parents.' Through all these years as housekeeper/cook here at 'Winter Forth' her love and devotion for Craig, Wilson, Lucy, and Jamie. Is just as strong as if they were her own children.' [Helen, reflecting back] 'for the last 8 months, Marcus has suffered with kidney disease. And on the 30th of June 2008 at 57 he unfortunately lost his battle and passed away.' [Craig announced] "in two weeks, there will be a wake for Marcus here at 'Winter Forth' out by the front garden." [two weeks later] Many people from Hillstem, arrived here. Amongst the crowd, I spotted four past guests of 'Country Life', one of them even asked 'do you mind if I say a few words during the service, in honour of Marcus?' It's a good thing there is plenty of outdoor space. Craig; "I thank you all for joining us on this sad day. "Where we lay to rest and honour our beloved Marcus. Our neighbor, a dear husband, friend, fellow worker. 57, still taken so young. "We met him when he was 29. When he began working here at 'Winter Forth' "I looked up to him like a cherished uncle". "He taught me how to groom a horse. "Most importantly though he shared this life lesson with me. "Which I'm going to share with you all. 'Persistence pays off!' "Marcus and his dear wife Meredith.

Celebrated their 7th wedding anniversary last September. "Those close to the couple would know. That their wedding may not have come about if he hadn't 'persisted.' "Earlier today, I recalled a conversation I had with Marcus in the past. "I'd like to re tell it to you. Provided no one else wishes to say anything..... waits. Ok, It was the 8th of August 2000. A month before their wedding. I sat right over there next to Marcus. [pointing out front veranda] "He was just smiling cheekily and giggling to himself. I asked what? What's so funny? "He said 'You know, I'll never forget the day, 'Edith' [what he called Meredith] 'Finally agreed to go on a date with me. I approached her, she was nasty, again! 'But this time, I'd finally managed to express all I wished to without being interrupted. 'No reply though. She just stood still looking at me. 'As if giving the impression, she didn't hear me at all! 'Then Edith [laughed] and responded with - [he paused] Craig [chuckled] I then asked him, "what? What did she reply?"

'Then Marcus said. She gruffly stated 'what took you so long?' Me and Marcus then smiled together. "He then told me, It took another 10 months, before she accepted his wedding proposal. [Laughs] "So friends, family and colleagues. 'persistence pays off.' R.I.P. Marcus Fletcher, you'll be dearly missed my friend, my brother." After the service people just talked amongst themselves, you could see Meredith was very overwhelmed. I did see Craig speaking with someone who later introduced himself to me as 'the produce padre' I imagined it was a reference to Vegetables and deliveries? Later that evening when everyone had gone home. I wondered, what became of Craig? I looked in the kitchen, sitting room, front veranda. Then I tried the back veranda. There he was sitting on the floral two seater swing, my parents gave us for our last wedding anniversary. I went and sat next to him. Then I said to Craig.

- "You know dear, I must plead ignorance on never taking the time to get to know Marcus better. Before... well. Just that, before it's too late. As the saying goes."
- "I know what you mean, if I had known him better. It wouldn't have come as such a shock. "To learn, he'd always wanted to go on a tropical sailing trip. Then retire in SA," Craig began laughing. "My dad told me, he sometimes teased Marcus, soon after he began working here." "Everyone could tell, he was infatuated with Meredith. So awkward and bumbling every time he saw her. "You could see it a mile away. Of course, when I said everyone! There was one, who had no idea."
- "really... Who was that?"
- "Meredith! She had no clue."

'The produce padre' told me the story today about Marcus and Meredith's first date. Let me tell you. [Craig narrating, as the Produce Padre. In his own words] "In town one day, Marcus felt unsure, insecure. "I told him, you need to just tell her how you feel man! "Marcus, got this horrified look upon his face. Marcus, shook his head, sighed and said 'I've tried mate, whenever I get the chance. I'd nicely begin talking to her. And each time Meredith was just plain nasty.' Helen and Craig [laughed] together as they could just imagine Meredith's stubbornness. Having been on the receiving end, multiple times themselves. Helen then said, "the padre, told you all this. He must have a good memory."

- "Yeah, I guess. They did catch up regularly. When Marcus went into town. Maybe it was multiple snippets of info. 'The Padre' fashioned into a story. "Marcus, himself once told me of a time in the past. "Where he approached Meredith. She was hanging out the clothes. "He was all intent on asking her to go with him to the movies? He called her name, [Craig laughing] Meredith turned around, threw a hand towel at him and said 'wash your face before dinner, will ya!' Then she walked back inside."

- "I tell you, the way those two would rile each other up. I'd thought for sure there would never be an attraction. A real cat and mouse scenario. "The kind people only read about. Those 'love to hate you relationships.'
- They laugh together.
- "We mustn't laugh at such things. We need to go and be of comfort to Meredith. Helen, give me your hand."

They stand up together. And head back into the kitchen. Meredith and Marcus lived in the very same small cottage that Malcolm Winter stayed in before the manor was built. Originally it was 18 foot long and 12 foot wide. Logan and Craig extended it soon after Helen moved in and is now 40 foot long and 25 feet wide. Two months have passed now since Marcus's funeral. Meredith got a surprise visit from her sister Louise. They stayed in her cottage together for three days. When Louise was returning home, she invited Meredith to come live with her in Adelaide. Understanding that she will be lonely now, Meredith regards 'Winter Forth' as her home and where her family lives. Well extended family and she wasn't comfortable with the idea of just leaving them. Or leaving the children. Besides, Meredith does have company.

She is responsible for Marcus's cat 'Mittens' and even if she did leave everything behind and accept Louise's offer. Meredith's own cat 'whiskers' would never forgive her for leaving her partner. Meredith and Louise spoke about spending a week or so together in Adelaide instead. But living there permanently was just something. Meredith wasn't ready for. Although it hasn't been easy for her, picturing Marcus in and around the farm. When he was gathering feed from the barn, riding the horses, mowing the grass, or tending to the gardens. Doing those things, always gave Marcus a sense of pride. Especially seeing how radiant the horses looked after their brushing. How vibrant the flowers appeared, days after watering. Marcus had such an infectious laugh. Anyone beside or close to him, couldn't help but to chuckle along. If they felt down, it'd pick their mood right up again.

Chapter Eighteen

⚘

August, 2008. Wilson reminiscing when he met Monique

With Monique being away for work. Wilson, happily accepted an invitation to dinner at 'Winter Forth.' Not only does it get him out of the house but he gets to spend some time with his niece, Lucy and nephew, Jamie. He'd planned on returning home after dinner but decided on staying the night. It had just gone 4 o'clock. Lucy and Mrs Sherwood were in the kitchen preparing dinner, Jamie was in his room. Chores are done, animals fed and settled. Wilson, tried to assist with dinner. And was quickly told by the ladies "we got this!" he went upstairs to Jamie's room.

- "Jamie, would you like to build something together with Lego? I'm sure we can create something even taller than last month's 'Ice queen's temple!'
- "I've got homework to finish, sorry uncle. Perhaps another time."

Wilson, returned to the kitchen, picked up his coffee and walked out onto the front veranda. He sat in a nearby wicker armchair. And found himself staring at the garden around the turning circle. Then he suddenly saw an image of a 12 year old Monique. Clear and as visible as if she were standing there for real. Wilson knew this was not possible. Monique is in Colorado, I just spoke with her two hours ago. Wilson looked a little closer, Monique is standing at the back of her parent's car. Her parents car! Alright, something is not adding up here. Wilson, rubbed his eyes and looked again. Darkness bar a few pathway lanterns. He said to himself. Whoa! That was weird. Then continued. Hang on! I know, what I was seeing. But how? I grew up here. No one had ever mentioned 'Winter Forth' is a magical place. I've heard of things like this happening before. Logan [Dad] looked out and around these grounds. Then clear as day. He saw how he met Renee [mum]. Craig was thinking about 'Winter Forth' when he flashed back on Russel's birthday. It was on the front veranda steps where Marcus, clearly recalled his first encounter with Meredith. And again, dad was over in the garden. When he spoke of first meeting Robert Evans. Lastly, it was out here. Just like I am now. Where grandma Marian told myself, Craig and Russell all about our Great, great granddad. Malcolm, Scott Winter. I always felt a deep connection to this place. But same as many people do when they think back or visit their childhood home. Wilson sat down again in the armchair and said aloud. "I wonder?" He closed his eyes and again pictured Monique. There she was. Standing by the back of her parent's car. Wilson said to himself. This is when her and her family were guests here at 'Country Life' bed and breakfast. Not only did people like staying here, but they enjoyed the true experience of 'life on the farm.' Things like hand milking, collecting eggs, feeding the chickens, feeding and watering the horses, harvesting fresh veggies. According to dad, he was asked on many occasions 'Mr Winter, can I take the tractor out?' Everyone loved the atmosphere. It was 'real country living, near a city.' 'Winter Forth farm' was open to guests, all year long. At the time, Dad had three horses and two ponies visitors could ride about the grounds if they wished. Though guests usually bought their own horses. I remember it was a clear Friday morning in September, 1991. The Connelly family arrived at 10am from Tempurst, NSW. As they pulled up. Mr & Mrs Connelly were in the front, you could see two passengers in the backseat. Stepping out of the left hand side was a little freckle faced boy, who looked about ten years old. He immediately begun running around. Then a young girl emerged from the right hand side of the car. She stood against the window of the door and retied her long brown hair, then shut the door. She was wearing a pair of brown boots, old blue faded jeans and a checkered red and black flannelette shirt. Mr Connelly called out to my Dad who came out to greet them. 'Where can I get some water mate?'

'Oh yeah, right around this way, you'll see a white tank.' Mrs Connelly, got out and headed to the rear of the car. Logan met her there and said 'don't trouble yourself with your bags Miss. My sons can help. 'WILSON! CRAIG! Out the front please!' called Logan. Wilson and Craig, promptly stood beside Logan. 'yes Dad?' 'Here they are ma'am. Please, boys help..... ah....' Motioning to the woman to introduce herself. Mr Connelly, interjects 'apologies, this is my wife Francis. Our Daughter Monique and that boy, carelessly hanging from the rail along that small bridge. Is our son Mark. I'm John, this beautiful light caramel horse here is (Malt) he belongs to Monique. The black pony with various white spots is (Hoppy) Mark's pony.' Logan instructs the boys to please take their bags down to 'Proudly Pure', room 2.' 'Proudly pure' consists of two family room apartments and two double room apartments. It features a communal kitchen, lounge room, laundry and a shared entertainment area. Wilson returned to the car, Monique leant down to pick up her carry bag. She heard a voice behind her saying 'I can take that, if you wish?' Monique, replied. 'its fine. Which way we going?' Wilson said 'just down the back here. We can take my horse, if you wish? Or we can walk?' Monique replied. 'This bags not too heavy, we'll walk.' 'Ok, follow me' replied Wilson.

- 'Here we are, should you need any help, the phone in your room can dial reception.' Said Wilson.
- 'Thanks, 'I'll let mum and dad know.' Monique replied.

[20mins later] Wilson knocked on Monique's door. She answered it, saw it was Wilson and said playfully 'I've been folding and putting clothes away since I was eight. I don't need any help.' They both laugh.

- 'No, it's just that we've still got some time before dinner. Would you care to join me for a ride around the property?'
- 'Sure, that sounds like fun. I'll meet you at the steps near where we pulled up.'

Her family is only staying for the weekend. Then they're heading back to NSW. 'You've got a really beautiful place here, beautiful fields, large open spaces.' said Monique. Their ride took about 20 minutes. Whilst heading back to Monique's room. Wilson pointed out he's favourite spot along the bank of the billabong. They pull up at the guest stables, dismount their horses and head inside. In the lobby, Wilson thanked her for the ride, then asked 'Could I have your phone number?'

- 'But, were leaving in a few days.'
- 'I know, but we could still text each other over the rest of the school holidays!'
- She giggled playfully, 'silly Wilson, your on holidays now, but I'm not yet. Queensland and New south wales remember?'[smiles]

Wilson looking embarrassed that he had not thought of that himself. He turned around feeling foolish. Monique put her hand upon Wilson's shoulder and said 'walk me to my room' Wilson stood just inside the door. Monique sat at the table under the window, she wrote on a piece of paper, folded it in half than handed it to Wilson. She hugged him and said. 'see you tomorrow.' then closed the door. Out in the hall, Wilson unfolded the note. It read 'Monique, 0428 675 453. After school and on weekends. Thanks for showing me your favourite place.' Wilson let out a deep sigh! He went outside, mounted his horse 'Gerard' and rode back to Winter Forth manor, [smiling] the whole way.

[Present day] There are just so many happy memories and good times here. Wilson, walked back into the kitchen. And Just as he sat down. The phone began to ring. Mrs Sherwood answered it. An excited Lucy called out "is that Mum?"

- "Oh, no my Pet. It's for your uncle."
- "Thank you, Meredith. Who is it?"
- "It's your wife, Monique."
- "hello darling [conversation] that's great! Was it who you hoped it would be?...., Excellent! No worries, I'll meet you there at 11am. I love you too, bye."
- "What is it Uncle Wilson?"
- "Well, your Aunty Monique is on her way home. I'll be picking her up tomorrow morning. Then we'll come back here for lunch."

Chapter Nineteen

❦

Christmas camping trip, December 2008

I t's boxing day, 8am. Today were heading off to Ashhern RV and trailer park. Where we will be staying for a week. Dad loaded up our family car, hooked up our 28ft caravan and informed us. "I want to be on the road by 11am." We planned places to visit, mum arranged a list of different places we can eat at.

A family favourite place to visit in Ashhern, is the museum. Mum came down the stairs. Placed her suitcase near the door along with a box from the kitchen. [9am] before mum sat at the kitchen table, she placed a letter for Wilson, on the bench near the door. Wilson, is more than happy to look after and run 'Winter Forth Farm' while were away. Before he married aunty Monique. There were times he came with us. Actually last year, Monique joined us as well. She only stayed for three days, then had to leave. Monique worked in the fashion industry. Often needing to travel out of town on business. Everyone, looks forward to her return. Because she says she has a celebrity story to share. Very mysterious about it and honestly they tend to get a little frustrating. It's almost like an audio only version of that popular family game 'Pictionary'. Monique, begins her excitement with a 'you'll never believe it! I saw ...., waiting in line at ....' or a 'wow! Do you know that .... is secretly dating......! She refuses, absolutely refuses! To mention names. Actually, I'm not 100% sure if it is a blunt refusal or a legal obligation? When she's getting ready to leave. Monique always appears really excited. It looks as though she's bursting to tell. But no! It is Frustrating, yes! But a professional approach none the less. Her only response remains 'discretion, my dears. Discretion!' Monique then walked outside, I know my mum followed her. Trying to as she put it "convince her to just tell her who it is!? And I promise not to tell anyone else." To my knowledge, Monique never told her. Only thing mum did relay of that conversation. Was that Monique, came right up close to her and whispered 'channel 9, 8.30pm tomorrow night.' [10am] Craig said to everyone "I thank you for placing all luggage near the door, it's a big help. Especially to you Lucy for your help and thank you, Jam.... Where's Jamie?"

- "Hmm? He was here a minute ago!"
- "I saw, Jamie. He's out by the garden, watching the trains as they rock on by."
- "ah! That boy, he loves watching those trains. Ever since he was younger. Lucy, please ask your brother to come inside." [Lucy and Jamie enter together]

I began to say earlier. "Thank you, kids for tidying up your rooms. Let's briefly go over agenda. "Ashhern, is a four hour drive. Upon our arrival, Jamie and I'll unpack the car. Lucy, please help your mother."

- "That'll be great Lucy. Once checked in, we can go for a walk together to the corner store."
- "Alright it's now [11am], let's go."
- [After settling in] Craig, asked everyone to gather around. Tomorrow [pause] I was thinking we visit t..-' Craig barely finished his suggestion. When everyone called out at

once in excitement 'the museum!' Ok the museum. Craig
agreed. Craig reminded his family that at 11am next Friday,
we'll be returning home. He then read out the places and
attractions available in the surrounding area. Which are;
Indoor rock climbing, the museum, hot air balloon.....
the –"

- Lucy interrupted 'What about the ....? you know! Mr
  McCarthy told us about it. Dad! You promised!
- "Ah yes of course, thank you Lucy. Horse jumping.... Craig
  went to continue. "There is also -.
- "Dad, that's not fair! If she can add horse jumping. Then I
  add the speedway!" adds Jamie.
- "Alright boy, here's what were gonna do. Places and
  activities, all get written down. We draw them out of a
  hat, do them in order they come out. One in the morning
  and one in the afternoon. [Helen hands over her hat]

Alright in they go. Craig, whispers to Helen [I added one
of my own, for you.] Mum, kissed dad and said "you're so
thoughtful."[smiles] Now we know the museum is tomorrow
morning. Afternoon is...? Helen reaches into the hat. "Saturday
afternoon will be Beach & BBQ. Then Sunday morning, indoor
rock climbing. Afternoon, speedway. Monday morning, Country
Craft fair [smiles at Craig, happily] afternoon, horse jumping.
Tuesday morning, hot air balloon ride. Afternoon, trip to the movies.
Wednesday morning, shopping spree, Afternoon, 'Poker Plate.' to
determine dinner choice. ['Poker Plate' Granddad Logan, invented
this. When he explained 'the rules' he told us. You can play with
anything you like. For example matches, coins, poker chips, buttons,
marbles or toothpicks.] Helen, Laughed. She remembered. Logan,
say he once knew someone who used 'monopoly money.' We use
5c coins, mum has collected over the years. She keeps them in an
old milo tin. Mum thinks she's so clever. 'Hiding them away' but I

know the tin is under the laundry sink. It is played the same way as any poker game. Only instead of winning money. We varied this, to a 3in a row winner. Winner chooses dinner or where we go for dinner. Thursday morning, Driving tour/picnic- seeing the sights. Afternoon a trip to 'Country Caring Sanctuary' then on Friday we leave.

[10am, next Friday] Much of the packing got done last night, so after an enjoyable, lake side breakfast. They're ready to leave. After leaving the trailer park, Craig automatically went to turn left out of the driveway onto the freeway. When Helen suddenly cries out "STOP!"

- "What, dear? What's wrong?" Craig asked worried.
- "I need us to turn right please!"
- "Where are we going to?"
- "just down the road a little."
- "And how many K's is a little...? Oh my goodness! We forgot something didn't we?"
- "No, we didn't forget anything. And I'm unsure, as to how far? Just now when I checked out. I was told, the sign went up, not long ago."
- "What if we get lost?"
- "Not possible. At the very least, we'll end up back at the 'Ashhern RV and Trailer park." Soothed Helen.
- Craig, confused. Asks "Sign? What sign?"
- "Our sign, remember?... Informing people of 'Country Life' Bed and Breakfast, accommodations available in Hillstem."
- "Oh! Our sign. That's great. Where did Harold say it was mounted?"
- "Uh, Harold didn't! Marianne did."
- "Marianne? She couldn't find both shoes, on her feet! I don't wanna have to drive for hours. In the wrong direction."

-    "she assures me 'it's not too far before our turn off the highway.' Look there's a sign for the trailer park. Slow down a little, hon."

Ok, turn around. We should see it on the return. There! I think I see on the second post. Pull over here dear. They park and all pile out. Lucy in front, says excitedly "here it is." Helen remarked, "What a great picture of the manor and a beautiful representation of the animals, the fields, windmill and the billabong. Craig then said. 'It's nicely worded too and reads aloud.' "Country Life' Bed & Breakfast. 'Winter Forth Farm'. Located 45min from Hillstem, QLD. Short or long term accommodations available. Book now and be welcomed by friendly hosts: Craig and Helen Winter." Phone: (07) 4614 7890 Mobile: 0428 147 890 or Email: countrylife.2017@hills.com.au

[Back home]

Logan asks Craig. "how was your trip, my son?"

-    "Excellent dad, we had a great time."
-    "I apologize again, I couldn't join you."
-    "We saw many attractions. I'll share with you the two most memorable. Saturday, morning we went to the museum."
-    "The museum! Again! Haven't you seen everything there?"

"Perhaps, none of us tire from the experience. We've gone there ever since the kids were born. We've seen the traditional exhibits. Yet every time, there is some new attraction to see. "A few years ago, "Jamie was absolutely fascinated with 'marine life.' Then last year, Lucy almost got left behind. "She just wanted to soak up everything about the dinosaur exhibit. We never have joined the tour group. "We know our way around there pretty well by now."

-    "What else did you really enjoy while you were away?"

- "The Saturday afternoon. Lucy and Helen walked along the beach. "Jamie and I hired a fishing boat. "We each bought things home. the girls, new dresses and us guys a bucket of freshly caught fish. "In the evening we had a family BBQ, homemade potato salad, garden salad and.... our deliciously looking caught fish."

Chapter Twenty

❦

Puppies

long the way home, Lucy and Jamie fell asleep. Once Helen turned into their driveway, they both woke up. Lucy, got out first. She hurried over to Uncle Wilson who threw he's arms around her. Then it appeared as he had whispered something in her ear. Lucy's face beamed with an ear to ear grin. She cried out excitedly "really!"

No one else heard what Wilson told her. But it was no doubt happy news. Not more than a minute had passed and Lucy came darting around the corner from the backyard. She ran straight up to Wilson, interrupting him and Jamie and anxiously asked "where? Where is she?" Wilson directed her to the front veranda. There was a quite content M&M, spread out nursing 7 puppies. Lucy called out to her mother

- "Mum!, Mum. Come and see how cute they are!" Lucy then asked Wilson, "When?"
- "Three days ago, four boys and three girls."
- "We suspected a pregnancy, yet it was unconfirmed."
- "I'll start thinking of names. I have an idea for this one, ooh! Lucy [giggles]
- Helen said to everyone "We've, um established the birth...... but uh my question is the..., the..., um...... Well, frankly

who? Jamie's dog, 'Fergus' is still a pup himself. So that's not possible."

- "It must have been that family whom stayed for four days, around 2 months ago."
- Dad, "what was their name?" [Lucy thinks] Was it Oscar? Or Oren?" Oh well. Im gonna go look at them again."
- "I don't recall their surname either. I remember their beautiful dog. 'Lefty' a bull mastiff. He had a light brown coat with dark brown paws, and a white patch above he's left eye. "That little sneak, I only ever saw them running along the billabong a couple of times. "The rest of their stay, they were a part. Hmm? Or so I thought."
- Craig commented to Helen. "Why is he the 'little sneak?' Did you think, It could have been M&M's idea?" [they laugh]

I am sure M&M, will be cosy enough. To remain here in the corner of our veranda. At least until I can make her kennel more comfortable. Helen asked "Lucy, tell me the names you've chosen, dear?"

- "Osbourne."
- "Osbourne? Queried a puzzled Helen. Strange name, seems more like a surname then a first name."
- "It just came to me, Osbourne was the surname of the family who stayed here. "I'll call the boys 'Dave, Titch, Twirl and Spotty.' And the girls, 'Daisy, Dee and Pixie.'
- "Those sound, creative dear. You know their new owners will rename them. "It is a shame we can't keep them all. Maybe one or two" said Helen
- "I know mum." replied Lucy.

Lucy is now 18, she's finished school and when she's not spending time with her friend Susan Wheeler. [farmer garth's granddaughter. right of winter forth.] Lucy and 'Shearer' are down at Mr McCarthy's ranch. Together they run his small jump course. When Lucy got home, she received a phone call from race official Mr Alex Fredricks. She could hardly contain her excitement. Mr Fredricks, officially invited her and 'Shearer' as past champions to attend the 200m race in Runegate. Lucy happily accepted and this coming Wednesday. They will be heading off. Unfortunately, 'Shearer's' racing days are behind him.

Though he will of course be paraded for the past winner he is. They did manage to enter a series 1 of competition jumping. Along with five other horses/jockeys. They'll be there a total of five days. 'Shearer' and Lucy have participated in four local events within the last five years, winning twice. Lucy's room displays trophies for jumping and racing. Some for 'poise' as well as her academic achievement trophies and awards. Lucy always was an excellent student. Her friends and team mates have commented to her on more than one occasion 'thank goodness your dad's a carpenter! You'll soon need more shelves for rewards' Craig, will be accompanying Lucy to Runegate. Helen is staying home with Jamie and she also plans on spending some much needed time with her Mother Becky. Wilson has offered to help out around the farm and Russell, Logan and Robert. Have things covered with work.

Off to the races, 10th June 2015

Logan walked 'Shearer' over to the trailer and Lucy threw the rest of her things in the back of the car, kissed her mother goodbye, hugged grandad Logan then took the reins off him and guided 'Shearer' the rest of the way in. "Be good, bro!" Lucy called out to Jamie. When they arrived at the caravan park, Lucy glanced around, to see if she recognized anyone. There were only two, Lucy knew when she saw their horse floats. She then said to herself. 'They were at the race, last year in Sagehurst.' Craig returned from the office and said excitedly to Lucy

- "You're all set kiddo. All registered, competitive jumping. Will be at 9am tomorrow morning."
- "Thanks dad, im just gonna quickly change my clothes."

[now changed] Lucy opened up the horse float, put the reins on 'Shearer' then walked him over to the stables. Lucy topped up the water, cleaned out the feed trough. And prepared to feed 'Shearer'. She reached down to grab a biscuit of hay. But grabbed someone's hand instead. Lucy let out a [squeal] and instantly jumped back, startled. [Soothing] 'Oh silly girl, Lucy. I must just be tired!' I don't actually believe there is anyone else in here! She stepped forward, reached up to place the reins upon the hook. Lucy then heard faint footsteps, Lucy looked behind her. No one there! Lucy, tries again to place the reigns on the hook. They were nearly there when she accidentally dropped them. Before picking them up, Lucy, could swear she hears rustling, and running water. Lucy let out a worried/anxious [sigh] then she bent down to pick up the reins. On her way back up. Lucy bumped heads with someone. [oow, ouch!] She placed her hand to her head then stood up fully and come face to face with whom she'd bumped heads with. This man, turned on his torch. Now Lucy, can see her victim. She realizes, she knows him. It was Louis, Louis Sutton. Who with his free hand was also holding his forehead. Lucy could hardly believe it was him. He looks as handsome as he did when they first met in 2013. Though he's black curly hair is longer, and appears he has early sprouts of a moustache. It's no wonder, I had trouble hearing him walk around.

Louis is lean and only 165cm tall. Now her eyes have fully adjusted to the light. Lucy, once again gazed deep into his brown eyes, whilst admiring his smooth olive skin tone.

- [smiles] "Are you ok?'" asked a concerned Louis.
- "Yes, I'm sorry, I didn't see you there."
- "Lucy, I didn't realise you were here a part of this event! Are you sure, you'll be alright?"
- "I'll be fine, thank you. I got here this afternoon with my dad, Craig. [laughs] "...um.... I still need to feed my horse. She [giggles] "I'm guessing that was your hand on the bale of hay?"
- "Yes, [laughs] I was feeding 'Sir Rufus'.
- Lucy pointed to her horse. "You remember 'Shearer'?"
- "Yes, I do. It's good to see you two again. I missed you.., ah I mean. You missed last year's competition."
- "mum and dad had to work. How did it go?"
- "Oh, well 'Sir Rufus' came third in the race and we placed second with the jumps"
- "who came first?"
- "Molly Western and 'Charlotte' for jumps. First place race winner was Henry Grady on 'Phoenix'."
- "Which van are you and your mum staying in?"
- "We're in no 4, all the way back there." [pointing to the far left corner]
- "Me and my dad are in 12. Down the front here. Speaking of dad, I'd better get back he'll start to worry. "Hey Louis, I have an event in the morning. When I come back. Would you be interested in a ride together along the lake?"
- "Sure, that sounds like fun. Just knock on my door. When you're ready."

Lucy opened her caravan door. And said "hey dad you'll never guess who I just ran into, well bumped! Into actually.

- "Louis Sutton. He's here with his mum. "Tomorrow afternoon, Louis and I are gonna go for a ride together."
- "alright, only, please don't be late in getting home... Remember... you won our 'Poker Plate' card game, Pizza it is!"
- [giggles] "That's right, I whooped your butt, with them three 9's. [they both giggle] I'll be back in time." Assured Lucy.

[Next day] Knock, knock. Louis opened the door.

- "You ready to go?"
- "yep! Where do you wanna go?"
- "First a ride through the park, then stop in at that café. You know, the one, right on the edge of the park?"
- "Oh yeah! [Remembering fondly] they served the best milk shakes."

They mount their horses. Ride on Shearer, commanded Lucy. Louis gives 'Sir Rufus' a little kick. Another fond memory came into Lucy's mind when she thought of that café. It was where she first met Louis, two years ago. The café was newly opened and the only close place to quickly duck in out of the rain. They tied their horses up outside. Walked in and sat down in a booth, adjacent the counter. [waitress appeared] Lucy began saying "could I please -?" Louis took over, continuing the order. "1 ham and cheese toasted sandwich and a regular chocolate milkshake please."

- Lucy smiled. "Only one sandwich?"

- "I'm not very hungry, thought we could share it. Besides, mum is doing a potato bake tonight."
- "sharing it is an excellent idea. I'd best not have a lot either. My Dad has to... [chuckles] ah, my dad is ordering us pizza. [12 mins later] "It really is good to see you Louis and thanks for the sandwich and drink [laughs] well half. [Lucy looks around] How about we ride home, via the lake? "The sunset reflecting off the water will be a beautiful sight."
- "I'd love that," He opens the door. "shall we?"

They got down off their horses and sit down together on the narrow stretch of sand that runs along the edge of the lake. No exaggerations. It truly was beautiful. The bright orange reflecting against yellow with a hint of pinkness amidst the grey clouds. Some trees scattered around, all with clear underbrush. If this isn't officially designated a 'romantic spot' it sure felt that way to Louis and Lucy.

- Louis [leaned in] took a hold of Lucy's hand and asked "is there anyone special in your life at the moment?"
- Lucy, shot Louis a stern look toward him. As if to state, [if there was! Would I suggest such a romantic spot?] Lucy leaned on Louis's shoulder [sighed] and answered. "No, just you. She smiled. They stood up together and hugged.
- "Lucy, would you mind if we came back here tomorrow?"
- "Tomorrow? But .... I have to..." Louis placed his fingers across her mouth [smiled] and continued, after your event and presentation."
- "Ok, that will be nice."

They ride back to the stables. Louis heads up to his caravan and just as Lucy goes to step inside hers. As they part company, Louis calls out "it's a date then!"

12th of June 2015. Race day.

[Morning] Lucy called out to her father. "It's time to go dad!"

- "Alright kiddo. Let's go. When we get there, you go to registry and I'll head up into the grand stand. Loading 'Shearer into the trailer. "Good luck to you both. [hugs] Lucy [ruffles up Shearer's mane]
- "thanks dad."

[all lined up at the gates] announcer; "Ladies and gentlemen, welcome to the 27th annual race day. All horses are in position ready to begin on my mark. 1, 2, 3 BANG! And there off!" [moments later] Announcer; [Mr Fredericks] "This was a very close one folks. With no '6' Willow. And no '7' Trotter running side by side much of the way. But in the end no '7' Trotter, was declared our first place winner. Rider, Terry Angus. '6' Willow, rider Brett Hawkes. Came in second. Third place was no '9' Charlotte, rider Molly Western."

- "Congratulations to you Mr Angus. And 'Trotter.' Please come up to the front my boy."
- Lucy, stood beside Mr Fredericks. Shook, Terry's hand. Said well done. Then said. "Would you please say a few words."
- Mr Angus, shook Mr Fredericks hand than stepped in front of the podium. [clears throat] "I'd like to thank my personal trainer, my parents. Especially my grandpa for always believing in me. Thanks to my fellow jockey's. Good race and congratulations to Brett and Molly." [raises up his medal] and returned to his seat.

[Back at the caravan park] Lucy is visiting with Louis and his mum Catherine, in their kitchen. "when are you two heading back to NSW?" Lucy asked.

- "In two days, my husband Frank is picking us up at Runegate train station."
- "I remember your husband Frank. How has he been? "Is he still working at 'McIntosh and Kline Lawyers'?"
- "Yes, that's why he wasn't able to join us on this trip. A big case between. Has all his attention. Its between Nicole.... And ..... Oops! Sorry, I'm not meant to talk about it. Anyway, I will say this. If things occur, as he said they should. He'll bring me back my personally autographed book, Ooh, I'm excited! She's my favourite author."
- "Is that the time 7.30pm? I'd better get home and help dad pack up. We leave tomorrow."
- "I'll walk you out, Lucy."
- "You have my phone number." They kiss each other goodbye.

Along the drive home, Lucy found herself remembering the day she got 'Shearer' [Lucy envisioning the story] Although I never shared my brother's fascination or love for trains. [smiles] I do fondly remember the passion, I had and still have to this day for horses. Recalling this great memory now. It's one of. No, it was and actually is one of my greatest memories. Jan 6th 2002, It was the morning of my 4th birthday. I woke up and noticed a large gift on the end of my bed. When I picked it up, I felt it was soft. My mind began guessing with excitement. It's those pink pyjamas, A towel or ... maybe a jumper? I tore it open, held up the item inside. As it unfolded, I saw it was a square blue cloth. [not knowing then what it actually was] I ran down into my parents room. Jumped up on the bed, hugged my mother. Happily saying to her, 'thank you for my tablecloth. I'm gonna set up the tea party.' I returned to my room.

- Mum [laughed] and explained. 'No dear, It's a horse blanket.'

- [Craig in the distance] 'Are you ladies, ready to go?'

Mum, dad and me got into the car. I didn't know where we were going or why. I know I was excited though. [Minutes later] we turned into Mr McCarthy's. He was standing on his porch, holding a broom.

- He called out 'Ah morning!', Mr McCarthy. Appeared friendly and welcoming. He walked up to me, offered out his hand and asked 'shall we, young lady?'

I looked at mum and dad, who agreed. I took his hand and we walked over to his horses. Mr McCarthy asked me 'which one, will it be?' As if to imply. I'd already made a choice, and we were there. Just to pick it up. I didn't answer. I Just looked at each one. There were four ponies. Two black, one chocolate brown and the other one appeared lighter brown, like caramel or a white coffee. Within seconds I answered.

- 'Mr McCarthy, I'd like 'Shearer' please.'
- McCarthy [confused] 'which one is 'Shearer' my dear?, That one!' He pointed to one of the black ones.
- 'The caramel one, brown hair, brown tail. White feet and white spots. On the right side.'
- 'Oh I see. You mean.... Mo..-'
- Lucy [interrupts] Yes, 'Shearer.'

From then on we spent each weekend together around our farm. I've had 'Shearer' just under a year now. One cool Saturday morning in May. I just packed away my dolls house, got changed and decided 'I'll go for a ride on 'Shearer.' When I got outside. I couldn't find him. I looked by the path that led towards the billabong. I looked out near the clothes line, checked around the right side of the manor. He sometimes likes to lay. In the shade near the bridge. Nope! I thought. 'I'll ask mum. So I ran back around the front and up onto the veranda. I opened the kitchen door. Mum was standing at the sink, washing dishes. I started to ask her. 'Mum, have you ...... - But mum cut me off.

- 'Well? Do you like it, my dear?'
- 'Like?,' I asked confused. I said, 'I'm looking for 'shearer.'
- 'Looking for! But 'Shearer' is with your..... and -.'

Craig calls out 'Lucy, honey, can you come outside?,' I walked outside, Dad came up to me and asked me to 'close my eyes and give him my hand.' I obeyed, we began walking. Near as I could tell. We were going to the garage. Instead of stopping there. We walked around to what would be the back of the garage. Dad, then called out to someone 'put the lights on please.,' Ok honey open your eyes.' I opened my eyes and there was 'Shearer', in a stall with a name plate on the beam above him. Craig then gestured with his right hand 'this is the stable we designed for shearer.'

- 'We?'
- 'Grandad Logan, Uncle Wilson and myself.'
- 'Oh! Dad, this is great.'

I felt like I was about to start crying. I [smiled] thanked and hugged each of them. Up until then 'Shearer' stayed off to the side of our carpark. I've no doubt, 'Shearer' loves his stable much better. Once I'd turned 10, [2008] we began entering local jumping competitions and some 'Pony Poise Parade' shows.

[Present day] around 2.00pm. Lucy sat up properly, just as they'd turned onto their street. Helen, just noticed the text message from Craig. Saying, 'we're nearly home my love.' She stood up from the armchair in the lounge room and headed into the kitchen. On her way Helen saw Lucy's dog Pixie. Who was one of the late

M&M's[sadly passed away, March 2011] daughters. Pixie was looking miserable laying at the foot of the kitchen door no doubt missing Lucy. You could just imagine what Pixie is thinking to herself 'this is longer then school, or shopping. Longer than going to Suzie's.' Pixie then rests her head upon her paws and lets out a small whimper. "It's ok girl, she'll be home soon." Helen's words didn't seem to perk her up at all. A slight tail wag of approval but she quickly replaced her head on top of her paws. Suddenly her left ear shot straight up and she was up on all fours, raced out the kitchen pet door, barking constantly and jumping around. Helen, eagerly watched her from the doorway, she knew what it was and saw the car approaching. When they pulled up. Lucy, barely got her feet on the ground and a pleased Pixie was all over her. "who's a good girl?" Lucy praised. She then grabbed her bag from the back of the car and came into the kitchen. Hugging her mother on the way. Lucy took her bag up to her room then returned to the kitchen. Lucy invited her mother Helen into the sunroom. Intending to have a 'chat' with her.

Chapter Twenty One

Telling mum about Louis

I sat down beside my mum, Helen. Who firstly asked, "where is your father?"

- "He is just putting 'Shearer' away"
- Secondly, Mum offered "join me in a cuppa?"
- "yes please."

While Helen was preparing the coffee's. Lucy, returned to her room to retrieve something she wished to show her mum. In the middle of the table I placed my ribbon for jumping. Mum bought the coffees in as she placed them onto the table she noticed my ribbon. Helen picked it up and said excitedly.

- "Oh my dear, that's wonderful, congratulations. "Remind me later to go congratulate shearer on his victory. I wish to hear all about your trip. "You know, your dad texted me. Apparently he 'had' to buy a pizza! "3, 9's hey! That's my clever girl. "You got those bluffing skills from your Granddad Logan. Helen laughs."
- I smiled, mum. "You'll never guess who was there?"
- "Oh! Wait, let me try um. Wally Atkins?"
- "No."

- "Sam Withers? That nosy girl, who believes everyone loves her? "Or was it Marian Wellard?"
- "No! See mum. I said you'll never guess. "Louis Sutton was there. "Do you remember him? He and his parents were guests here, almost two years ago. "Anyway, Louis was there with his mum, unfortunately his dad couldn't join them he's working. "Oh mum, it was really good seeing him again."
- Mum, noticing my [smiling and blushing] as I mentioned Louis's name. Asked
- "What else is Going on with that smile, Lucy Winter?"

I [sighed] "mum, he's just as cute and adorable as when we first met. Apparently he feels the same about me. "Imagine after all these years. I mean I was almost 16, we haven't called or written consistently since then. "Now, I'm almost 19 and he's 21. "Mum, he wants us to date. I'm not even sure how that would work? I mean. "I definitely still wish to attend TAFE in Sagehurst. "I'm not worried though, because I can continue my studies in NSW just as easily. "Louis is flying up in two weeks for a visit. "Is it ok mum? Please say it's ok! He'd only be staying for a week. "Uncle Wilson, could pick him up from the Airport."

- "You're a grown woman Lucy. You don't need my permission. Of course, he's welcome to stay here. We always have room, well usually. It'll be great you two spending some time together."
- "Thanks mum. I'm going to call him. [5 mins later] Louis said he's looking forward to his visit."
- "Hey Lucy, you said airport? Louis won't miss his car while he's here?"

- "No. he doesn't have one yet. Besides it's just for the week mum. We'll most likely be around here. If we need to go to town? I'm sure dad will lend us his ute."

Two months later August 2015

"Mum! Where are you..." An excited Lucy, rushes into the lounge room. "Yes, dear just here." answered Helen. [Turning off the TV] "Mum... I just got off the phone with Louis. He'll be here tomorrow afternoon. Mum, he wants us to live together..... here at Winter Forth. Can you believe that? He's bringing his horse 'Sir Rufus'! He bought a car for us and is borrowing a friends horse float. I'm so happy mum, Once we get settled in, I'm gonna head over to visit grandma and grandad." Helen, looked worried.

- "I really am happy. Mum. I'd hoped you would be happy for me too."
- [sniffs] "I am happy honey. It's my mother."
- "Grandma Becky, my gosh! How selfish of me. I meant to ask earlier if you'd heard from her?"

Grandad Jerry told us that last Tuesday evening. She had another fall. There's a little bruise on her knee, and hip. Nothing broken, thank god. For the next few weeks, My sister, Mary said she'll happily stay at home with mum. Until my dad gets home from work.

Chapter Twenty Two

Helen's mum, September 2015

Early in the morning, Helen gathered up fresh ingredients from their garden. She put on some music, then began preparing a salad for lunch. Mrs Sherwood, came up behind her, tapped her on her shoulder and said "Helen, your father is on the phone." She obviously, missed the phone ringing. "Thanks, Meredith." Helen, wants to be overjoyed in hearing from her father. Despite the old adage 'no news is good news.' But she struggled to stay positive of late. Especially since her mum [Becky} had her specialist appointment.

- Hi Helen, mum's able to slowly walk around, go to the toilet and bathe unaided. That bruising on her hip. Hasn't gone down. "Apparently it's just due to her diabetes and they say 'it's normal with the medication she's taking.' "Your mum appears to be in reasonably good spirits a lot of the time. "But I can sense when looking at her that the pain she feels is uncomfortably strong. The specialist, has ordered X-rays.
- "But if there were no breaks. Wouldn't that be pointless?"

- "Your mum's condition may be worse than originally thought. Due to the placement of the bruises, x-rays may reveal something more like a fracture."
- "Thanks for your call dad."

Helen, stared off blankly out the kitchen window. Closed her eyes and reflected back to three weeks ago, at Becky's house. Helen, Craig, Lucy and Jamie, arrive. They are greeted on the porch. Becky hugs Lucy and Jamie, then directs them to the kitchen [whispering] I just got some biscuits out of the oven. Helen hugs her mum. Becky then asked, 'how are you two going?' Helen replied, 'we're more interested in how you're doing?' Mrs Hewitt's mother mentioned to me. You missed water aerobics class Monday night. 'Oh, that Anne. She worries. [smiling] 'I have just seemed to struggle lately and found, I'm a bit more tired. When doing tasks I normally do or attend usual activities.. All I think of is 'how much longer? Can I just go home?' in the past, these have always been things I look forward to doing. But goodness me, dozing off at church, shopping takes me twice as long, I stand still, during water aerobics. 'Alright mum, well you let me know if I can help you at all?' Becky, [clears throat, coughs] and replies. 'No, it should be ok dear. Your dad's here. You take care of my grandchildren, im fine.'

[present day] knock, knock. Helen, opens the door and sees its her dad, Jerry.

"Afternoon dad. Please come in," they sit at the kitchen table. "I'll just get us a cup of tea." Said Helen. "We saw Dr Walker this morning. He is admitting your mother to a care village. "He believes this would be the best course of action for both of us. Soothing he said 'I've done everything I can do for her at home.' [hands him, he's tea] I'll be moving her in there this afternoon. Good news, the 'Charlize Christian Care Village' provides the level of daily care, treatment and exercise your mum will require. Bad news, it's 20kms out of Sagehurst.

- "How did mum take this?"
- "She understood, we were both pleased it was unnecessary to buy the room. They have units available for lease. Mostly used by patients whose carer's are in respite or 'stayover patients.'"
- "Please dad, if there is anything, either of you need? Just let me know."
- "Thanks love, I will. We should be fine though... although... Actually dear, there is something you may be able to help me with today? "I'd like to borrow that small TV from your lounge room."
- Helen appears [puzzled] she doesn't recall another TV in the lounge room. She says, I'll be back in a minute, I'm gonna check. Comes back and says dad, I don't see a TV! The only one, we have is our 42" in the entertainment unit.
- Jerry [shifted in his seat, sighed] and asks did you look in 'my hat stand...?'
- Helen still [confused]
- Jerry says. "Ok usually when were ready to go. I always ask 'Where's my hat?'
- Helen instinctively answers, "it's on your stand!" [they laugh] I got it now dad. She [giggles] the cupboard under the back window. "It has a TV in it! Huh, I never knew that!"
- "Yes, he answered. "I've placed my hat on there for at least a year. Same spot, usually has a cover over it. "A few months ago, I nosily peeked inside. That's when I saw the 25" TV. "Do you know if it works? Or is anyone planning on using it in the future?"

"Using it! Dad, I didn't even know it was there! Mrs Sherwood, may know more about it? Could be from one of the guest rooms?.... Wait, dad you said 25? "I remember now we bought that for Jamie. Around 16 months ago. He became obsessed with a nature series on whales? "It was strange. From the moment, Jamie could walk up the driveway by himself. we heard everything about the regular trains he'd seen. "Yet for two whole weeks, he barely spoke of them.

-   "If I recall correctly. It was for a school project!"
-   "Well no one could watch anything else. Especially when he binge watched. [laughs] "I'd forgotten that, I'm not even sure if he finished them or not? He achieved an A for the project. "If you don't mind me asking dad. Why do you need a third TV at home?"
-   "It's not for home, I'm allowed to provide your mother with a television. At the care village."
-   Ah! I see, let me speak Craig. He should be in agreeance. I'll have him bring it to your house tomorrow."
-   "Alright my dear, I'm gonna head home. Thank you for the tea. Where's my hat? That's right, he [laughs] I'll get it!

[two weeks later] Helen walked into their lounge room, sat down she put her hands to her face and [wept], Craig come over and sat beside her. "What's wrong dear?" She didn't respond. Craig, placed one arm around her and said [gently] Helen.. [Sniffling] she looked up] and says. "I just got off the phone with my dad. Dr Walker, told him my mum has 3-6months. [cries]. Dad's returning to see mum tomorrow and suggested I go with him (weeps). "What am I going to do without her? Hon, she's my mother, my best friend." Craig hugs her. Then soothed, "I'll go with you." Helen continued... "For as long as I can remember. Mother and I were always close. "Do you remember those yearly weekend shopping trips she and I took to Runegate. [laughing, reflection] Within an hour of arriving, mum insisted we go grocery shopping. Then enjoy a nice swim. Then over dinner, we talked about what each of us will buy tomorrow. "by dessert, just for fun we spoke of outfit or items we wished we could buy, if we'd won the lotto. Helen looked up closed her eyes, then continued. We always had a good time in Runegate. Well not just there, every place we went. [crying] "I.. just never... thought that trip, we made... last November. Truly, was our last one." [sighs, sniffs] Craig held her and replies. "I guess no one really thinks on those pesky, what ifs? Once realized, it's then too late huh?"

Chapter Twenty Three

Visiting mum

At the care village, they have a policy. Where no more than three people are allowed to visit at any one time. As we took turns, plenty of catch ups happened out in the waiting room. On more than one occasion some of us ducked away and returned with takeaway. I remember when it was mum's birthday. Everyone spread out in an undercover area near the garden. As people went home our numbers diminished. We were given free use of the conference room. Then when dinner was announced. Mum went back to her unit. I found myself at various times throughout the day. Just watch as she interacted with us all. Distant relatives, old friends, neighbours. Some cousins, and an uncle, I'd not seen for at least 4 years. Three past guests, had visited and caught up with Jerry. It's obvious that mum's mind is as sharp as ever. Only to express it as she does. 'it's my body, that's misbehaving!' As we were packing up the car, ready to leave. I thought, what a wonderful laughter filled day. Memories made and relived. I had difficulty believing the woman, I now know is calmly dosing off to sleep in her armchair. Is the same women who always insisted on walking over and exploring craters at an oceans edge, in her bare feet. Jumping up and over each crashing wave that hit the shore. [smile] In fact I believe it [giggling] was mum who announced loudly and confidently, "there is no wave, you cannot go over!" Through countless wipe outs, flops, and paddles back to the shore. [ah mum] Her ability, determination and confidence to stand by this announcement. Tackling those higher ones. Put those of us who opted to 'build sandcastles' to shame. [Back inside] Craig informed me, were ready to go. I went over to mum, [gently] tapped her on her shoulder. "Mum we're going now." Becky rouses [yawns] and says 'It was good seeing you my dear, would you mind topping my water up? And points to her glass. Helen fills the glass, turns to hand it to her mother. [who is resting again] Helen touches her gently on her shoulder, and says "Mum, Mum here's your water!" [No response] Becky, just turned onto her side. Helen leaned in closer to her mum and said "I'll place it on your bedside table." Kissed her mother on the cheek and gave her mother a hug.

Chapter Twenty Four

No improvement

(F our days later) Jamie called out. "We're almost ready mum!" "Ok, lad. We leave at 10!" Jamie joins Helen in the kitchen. "10? Why can't we go now? Can't we go now?" Helen suddenly got that all too uncomfortable feeling in her stomach [the one that usually means bad news.] "Well my dear, at the moment. Grandma is with Aunty Mary and grandad Jerry." Helen looked up at the clock on the wall. It read 9am. Still feeling worried. Helen decides to get last night's dishes done. [sighs] That should pass the time. Dishes rinsed, loaded into their dishwasher. Helen again checks clock, 9:15. She sits down [thinks] Craig hasn't returned from town yet. If we left now, he can meet up with us later. Umm, no. I'll give him another few minutes. Helen, stood up again, walked into the sunroom and begun folding the basket of laundry. Picked up the first item to fold but then was interrupted by the phone. On her way to answer it, she immediately started [fretting] "oh no it's Craig, he's going to be late."

- "This is Helen Winter, may I help you?"
- "My name is Catherine, I'm from the medical centre, I'm looking for Jerry McKenzie. His wife has not shown up for her appointment."
- "Jerry is my father, you've called their daughter, Helen!

- Uh, ok…. Sorry about that. I'd just like to know if I should reschedule? -"
- Helen (interrupts) "Please, Catherine. "My Mother?"…. Is she…?
- [silence]
- Catherine….?, thanks. I'll call my dad. Then I'll have him call you back"

Helen calls her father Jerry [ringing, ringing] answers "hello?"

- "Dad it's Helen. I'm calling because I just received a call from the medical ………."
- oh, Helen my dear. I'm sorry. I meant to call you before that happen. Your Mum passed away early this morning.
- "Oh my goodness! Dad, [weeping, sniffs] this is [teary] the call I've been dreading for weeks now."
- "It's lucky you caught me actually. I haven't used my mobile this much since I first got it. From being informed this morning, "I've had 3 phone calls back to back. Have been in and all around the Administrators office. She's only now being moved to the Hospital."
- [Calmly] "Alright, dad. You travel safely. With this wet weather around. We'll see you at the Hospital soon."

Helen called Craig's mobile, no answer- it went to voicemail. 'Craig, dad just told me mum's passed away. I'm heading to the hospital. "Wilson, is staying here with the Jamie and Lucy. Please meet me there. Love Helen.' [Next day] Helen went and visited her sister, Mary McKenzie. Together they wrote this article for the local newspaper;

McKenzie, Becky, Marie [nee Cook]
14/06/1943-07/01/2016 aged 73 years old

Helen Winter and Mary McKenzie, sadly announce the passing of our Mother.

late of 'Charlize Christian Care Village,' Sagehurst, QLD. Formally of Hillstem, QLD.

Becky is the beloved wife of Jerry, a cherished mother and dear grandmother to Lucy and Jamie Winter. A dear friend to all. She will be dearly missed. A memorial service will be held for Becky McKenzie at Hillstem Community Church on the 14th of January 2016 at 11am

Chapter Twenty Five

Becky's funeral

- "LUCY!, JAMIE! Come on you guys, into the car please.
- "Mum, I'm not sure about this dress!" stated Lucy.
- "Dear you look beautiful."
- Lucy hesitates.
- "What is it?"
- "It's just a lot of people are going to be there, some I know. But others we've not seen for years."
- "I understand, my love. It'll be okay. Stay close to me and dad. We need to stay strong for Grandad Jerry and Aunty Mary."
- "Yeah alright Mum lets go."
- "Oh and Lucy, don't forget to grab those flowers you prepared earlier[smiles] I love how you put the purple ones in the centre. They were your grandma's favourite."

Helen was so pleased with the church service for her Mother. She felt so [overwhelmed] every which way she turned or stepped someone gave her a hug or kiss. Or words of comfort. She remembers thinking with such [praise, admiration] how much Lucy and Jamie have grown up. Their so mature. Helen, is so very proud of how strong they've been. They've supported me, their cousins, friends, townspeople. Many people gathered here to celebrate

Becky's life and support Jerry. Jerry, Craig, Wilson, Russell, Jamie and Louis, were pall bearers. Everyone fell in behind them leaving the church. Then those who wish to will join us for a graveside service at 'St Augusta's cemetery,' Hillstem.

[graveside] Minister Pearce, invited anyone who'd like to share. To come forward. Jamie stood up. "My grandma Becky was very creative. Painting, drawing. Her compassion, kindness and determination. These are the traits she was well known for. As many of you saw, experienced. "As her grandson, I heard her tales of jumping over and riding waves at the beach. I saw her Sunday morning frustrations. "When quote 'granddad, didn't complete the crossword again!' The [upset] of her dogs refusing to go outside. "Not so well known to everyone was her personally written poetry. Fortunately, I was close enough to her to have heard some. "Together we created short ones. I'd like to share one with you now. Becky wrote it in 2005. [A tribute to her mother] "Grandma read this to me when I was 9. And from then until now, it remained unfinished. "We had planned to write the ending together. I'm not as vocal, or as expressive as she was but [looking up] grandma, [teary] "I finished this last night in honour of keeping our promise."

'Lost, found, and unbound.' By Becky McKenzie and Jamie Winter.

A day will come
where somehow
my smile alone will no longer succumb.
I'll be going through loneliness as before
Yet different to now.
Hope, fear. Will be at an end
no more sorrow.
Happiness, hope and love for each tomorrow
I now know why you gave up so?
it hurt you to watch me

throw
to the wind, all care discussion
and consideration. That I just couldn't show.
When turning my back on we,
I never heard or embraced your glee.
while walking away,
I never cared we'd be going our separate way!
My mums words, repeat in my ear.
He's good for you, so keep him near.
That's all she wrote, I added;
I'm forever thankful for good outweighing bad
love should be uplifting and kind.
With negative emotions minimal,
Always happy over sad.
By the sunset of every night
as with the dawning of each new day.
Your name is first and last on my mind
though at times I'm fierce, like an animal
thankfully it's never a serious fight.
I'm forever comforted, seeing your smiling face.
Remember wherever we are
Love, friendship will be a feeling we embrace.

Jamie, sits back down. Minister Pearce, thanks Jamie for sharing that with us. Her granddaughter Lucy, wishes to speak. Hugs Jamie on her way past.

- "Grandma, we will remember you dearly. I know you never would have wanted us to worry. "Which is why you never showed just how much you were hurting. Looking through my closet yesterday, searching for what I'd wear today. "I found the jumper, we knitted together. [laughs] I held it up and you know what? "Years later, grandma. You were right. It's true! The three colours I chose. Really didn't complement each other. "Also the pattern I cut, was twice my size. [smiles] I then I heard your soothing words 'dear, if you like it! it'll work.' "Thank you for always encouraging me with my schooling and confidence.

- Jerry, came up next. [Hugged] Lucy as she returned to her seat. "I thank you all for being here today, Becky would have truly been touched as I and my daughters are. Then he stated 'if anyone else cares to say anything? "Please come forward."

[Pause, silence] [looking around] no one else came up. Jerry continued, "we've hung a basket of short purple flowers here. [indicating to his right] They were Becky's favourite. "You're all welcome to walk by and place one on Becky's coffin." Jerry picks up the first flower, kisses it then places it on the coffin. He then took his seat next to Helen. Father Pearce, returned to the podium. He instructs the funeral director to play Becky's favourite song in the background. 'You'll never walk alone' by Gerry & The Pacemakers. People slowly approach, place their rose and sprinkle dirt. [music is turned off] Father Pearce, "please join us as we recite 'the Lord's prayer" [Jerry] "You're all welcome to join me and our family for some refreshment and reflection at the local RSL Club." Upon arrival, those that have not yet signed the memorial book are encouraged to do so.

There are two small tables, positioned below one of the double bay windows. On the left is the portrait of Becky [that was atop of her coffin, during the ceremony.] On the right there is a small laptop, scrolling various photos and videos of Becky throughout her life. The dining tables were arranged in a circular format, everyone seated can see a small round table in the middle. In its centre, there's a large pot. Only it's not a tree. Trunk and branches only. All around the base of the pot are different coloured paper leaves. Green, light green, yellowy green. A cup with black markers in it as well as a box of wooden pegs. People were encouraged to pick up a leaf, write one positive word, or one happy memory regarding Becky and peg it to its branches. Helen told Lucy, all about this display. They both remarked "I've not seen anything like this before. What a cool tribute." Lucy said, "come on mum. Let's write ours together. It isn't necessary to put your name." Lucy added. Helen approached the tree, one top branch was almost full. A second branch wasn't far behind. She picked a yellowy green leaf, pegged the peg to her shirt. Holding her leaf in her left hand. Helen, then began reading others leaves. She read 'humorous', 'loving', 'great cookie maker', 'devoted friend', ' my bestest friend', ' fishing in Runegate', 'proud mother' and one that gave her the widest smile yet. It read 'my wife, for life.' Helen, leant down and wrote 'my travel companion, my soul sister. Lucy wrote 'greatest grandmother,' love always Lucy."

Chapter Twenty Six

❦

Returning to work 22nd of July 2016

2pm, Craig was sitting in the kitchen having morning tea. Mrs Sherwood, appeared in the door way. Announced, "Russell is here!" Russell then happily asked "Are you ready mate?, he then added, a lovely morning isn't it!" Craig looked up with a [confused] look on his face. He repeated to Russell. "Ready...? – [seconds later] Craig said "Oh, Wednesday. We're off to Tempurst. Sorry mate, "I won't be a minute. Things have been a little hectic around here of late. I am happy to get back to work. "Helen's been staying with her dad, the last few weeks. They've been tidying up, you know? Alright let's go, I'll let Mrs Sherwood know." Heading down the driveway, Craig is driving. He asks Russell "how are Cherry and the kids doing?"

"They're good. Cherry is at home with our children. She managed to get some time off. Well as much time as any writer can have off. [laughs] "You know, I watch her around our house. She laughs out loud to herself, talks things through. She suddenly cries out, statements like. 'That'll be brilliant!' Or 'That scene will be even sexier if I ......' followed by more giggles. "I tell you bro, she really gets right into them romance, and passionate scenes she writes. "I'm not insecure or anything, but If I didn't know any better.

"I'd say those things really have happened to her. "The long laughs, sitting up during the night. Just having to secretly write. "Not to mention the blushing. They each appear so real, like an actual memory."

-   "Our appointment isn't until 10am tomorrow morning. It'll take us about 7-8 hours, before we arrive. I've got this for now. Feel free to relax mate, I'll rouse ya, [playfully slaps Russel's leg] when I need you to drive."

Russell, slightly reclined his seat, closed his eyes and began drifting off. He's first thought was. I'm gonna miss Cherry. The poor girl, she's been feeling upset ever since attending Becky's funeral. It unfortunately reminded her of how just a year and a half ago. Her own mother passed away, losing her battle with breast cancer. Russell, let out a [sigh, smiles] my Cheryl, how in the world did she pick me out of everyone to be her one and only love? [reminiscing] when I first met, Cherry. I was in year 8. And at that time, I wasn't looking to be dating anyone else. Not since my relationship with Leanne had just unexpectedly ended. Her mother became the new hospital administrator so Leanne and her family moved to Hillstem from NSW. We knew getting involved, that her mum could be relocated in 6-12 months. But we just couldn't be deterred. At first, we just studied English and science together. Next came close inseparable friends. I never was fascinated with science as a subject. But If there was a science team, whose primary goal was to turn a 24 hour day into a 25 or 26 hour day. I would have eagerly signed up, worked day and night. Just so me and Leanne could spend even more time together. [turned] Russell's head is now leaning against the car window. He continues reflecting. I remember, it used to take me weeks to muster up the courage, that was needed to approach a girl. Let alone speak to. Next week is the end of term. An excursion to the cinema has been planned. This will be perfect! I thought. During our study session this afternoon. I'll ask her to sit with me during the movie. What's the worst that could happen? Hmm, I mean besides getting a no! I entered the library and sat down opposite Leanne. We open our books, [smiling] I looked directly at her and begin 'Leanne will you?' She then said 'in reference to how we use the English language. 'Why do you think, we should use corrective sentences?' she thrust her ruler in front of me. Implying an interview scenario, with a microphone [ruler].... She repeated, 'Russell, why should we use corrective sentences?' [holding the ruler nearer to my mouth]

- 'I... [clear my throat] sat up straight. Ah, because. They make us sound so sophi..... Uh no, that's silly! Forget that! I'll start again. 'Alright Leanne. Here's an example of how and why corrective sentences, should be used! 'One could simply say 'come out with me!' Or perhaps this "corrective" structure, sounds better? 'Leanne, would you please accompany me to the cinema Friday night?'
- She smiles, puts the ruler to her own mouth and replies, 'good job Russell firstly, the second one definitely sounds more corrective. [giggles] placed her ruler on the table. Secondly, 'yes I'd love to accompany you to the cinema on Friday.'

[Friday morning] I can hardly wait. After 4 months of awkward stares, study meets, having lunch together. I'm going on a date with Leanne. I want to talk to her.... 'Only I didn't see her at attendance. 'It's ok, I'll see her in first period English. Everyone called out 'here' no Leanne. 'She must be running late or unwell. [1pm, looking at phone] no messages. 'Well, I'll see her later this afternoon. [4pm, knock, knock.] no one come to the door. I messaged Leanne, saying 'I'm here, on your porch. Are you ready?' [buzz, buzz] A message from Leanne, reading to himself. 'I'm so sorry, I couldn't tell you in person. 'Mum got relocated this morning. 'We headed back to NSW, to look for a house. I couldn't even say goodbye to you. 'My mum has dreamt of an opportunity like this for about 5 years now [management] 'I'll miss you, Russell. And I hope we can keep in touch. All my love, Leanne' The next two months seemed especially dull, I did enjoy receiving a letter, a post card and occasional text message. The hardest part was seeing her empty chair in front of me. As well as daily wondering 'if this pain will ever disappear?'

- "Russell!," Craig shaking Russell's leg. He sits up yawns. And asks "what's up mate?"
- "Would you mind driving for a bit mate?"
- "Sure."
- "There's a truck stop, coming up. Well grab some snacks, coffee then change seats. Give me 2.., 2 and a half ish hours. Then I should be right the rest of the way."
- "Sweet."

Russell stirs Craig. Hands him a cup of coffee and asks.

- "Are you ok to drive again mate?"
- "Yep all good. How long we got to go?"
- "About an hour."

Russell Meeting Cherry.

Russell settles back down into his comfy, familiar spot, he leaned up against the window and was able to drift back into his reminisce. What was I thinking last? Oh yeah, I wondered if my pain over losing Leanne, would ever disappear? The following Monday, I was running a little late, I turned up five minutes into my first class. Everyone had already taken their seats. Including my seat, it had been filled. I walked straight toward my desk and said.

- 'Excuse me Miss, that's where I usually sit.'

This young woman turned about in her chair, her curly auburn hair brushed across her face. And a pair of green eyes were looking straight at me.

- she smiled, then said. 'My bad it was empty when I got here. But you can sit here if you wish.' Motioning to the seat left of her.
- I said 'thanks', and put my bag on the floor.

Then the teacher, not so subtlety called out 'thank you, for joining us Mr Thompson!' [classmates laugh] That afternoon, heading down to the bus. I was surprised to once again see this beautiful seat stealer. She was walking straight toward me.

- 'I'm sorry about this morning. I'm Cheryl Winston, but please call me Cherry. We just moved here last Friday from SA. Cheryl, looked at me, as if to say [and you are?]
- 'Nice to meet you Cherry. I'm Russell. And as you may have gathered from our teacher, officially "Mr Thompson." [smiling, both chuckling] 'I'd better let you go now. You don't want to miss your bus.'
- 'Thanks, but I'm a little confused. I need 'Stokes' but I don't see it here. It should be 1, 2.. –'
- Russell, chimed in. 'bay 3' they said together. Are you sure, you need 'stokes'? I take that bus too.'
- 'Really! You're kidding?'
- 'It's absolutely true. I've taken that bus since year 1.[smiling]
- Cherry (giggled).
- 'Yeah, normally it is here. Today we got bay 2. 'Rooney' Our bus isn't running due to maintenance.'

We sat next to each other the whole trip home. Well that is until she got off. Guess where? The street, just before mine. Cherry is the next pick up after I get on and the last drop off before I get home. The rest as people say is history. [Shaking gently] "Come on mate, we're almost there. It was Craig's voice. He asked me to "look in the glove box for him." Then he pulled over.

- "Helen, put the hotel brochure in there for us. I need the address for 'Blake House'."
- Russell sat up straight and begun his search. "Yep here it is 'Blake House' "Ok, once we get onto Lewis street. "We continue along it about 120km until we see Richards Road. "Should be a right hand turn! "Unless …… You've already passed it!"
- "No, at the 'T' intersection we just past, "I turned onto Lewis. "Then I pulled over."
- "Ok, Lewis Street goes in both directions. "Let's turn around. Head back through and try turning right. "If I'm reading this small mud map right. Richards Rd, should be the third left."
- "And if you're reading it wrong?"
- "We uh? Uh. Turn round, try again. Going left this time. To be safe, we could put address in the GPS on your phone."
- "Brilliant thinking bro! Except phone battery died an hour ago. I'll read the street names as we pass and you confirm. [start the car again] First street, is Williams. Second street Oxley. Third …..- cross your fingers…. Richards. Ah ha, well done Russell. Just don't ever tell me where other mud maps have led you!" [giggling]
- "Slow down mate. The second right should be Blake Court! Swan….. Blake Court. "The hotel is 'Blake House, 12-16. Turns brochure upside down. [focusing] right at the end of the cul-de-sac."

- "Thanks mate, here it is Blake Court. Craig pulls up and parks their car. He then asked Russell, "where were you mate? Where did you go during your nap?"
- Russell got out stretched had a yawn. "Hmm? Oh high school. "Study sessions with Leanne."
- "Ah, the one that got away!"
- [raises his right hand] and says "not quite, she had to leave!"
- "Still.. ! Come on mate. "No need for sadness. As I recall correctly? "Shortly after that you met Cherry. "That's a happy ending my friend."
- Russell [shrugged] "You know Craig, meeting her. "Was also when I discovered. I can indeed love again. [smiles] "Real good times they wore."

[in the restaurant] Russell and Craig order dinner. Russell says, "remind me, we have our scheduled appointment tomorrow. "Then what?" [ring, ring] Russell answers his mobile. Its Cherry. "Hi honey, [amazed] then says lovingly. "That is strange, I was just thinking of you."

- "Oh! I hope it was in a good way?"
- "Yes, though it did involve Leanne."
- "Hmm, I see. I remember her."
- "What was that dear, I'm having trouble hearing you."
- "Yeah sorry, storms and heavy rain here at the moment. "It's actually why I'm calling..."
- "Let me guess, the children are spread out all over our bed. "Leaving you no room!"
- "Yes, that's incredible. Wait, naturally you'd know that. "Being an on hands father."
- "Sounds as bad as that big storm around 7 months ago. Kids were scared. Especially Joanna. Only you were out of town."

- "Russell...., I have tried 4 times to move them. 'They just huddle closer together. I just want to lay down. Just now. When I tried again. Bradley [5] woke up. And kept repeating the same thing over and over again to me." [Yawns]
- "What did he say?"
- Sighs, "What did he say? Oh yeah, he said 'Mr Thompson's Chair'. "He said it like four times! 'Mr Thompson's Chair'! "What is he asking for Russell? I need to know this? "It seems like the only item, that will coax them back into their beds! It's why I called."
- "Sorry dear, you're becoming muffled again."
- "Alright, I'll move away from the window..... Is that better?"
- "Yes, thank you. You were saying?"
- "Here at our house. "We have dining chairs, patio chairs and desk chairs. Its doing my head in. "I know of no 'Mr Thompson chair? Not even in your office. "Please..., Russell. "Where can I find it? [yawwwwn] I want to go to bed."
- Russell [laughs] "It's not what you think Cherry."

[waitress] here guys, we have one lasagne and chips and veg and one 250g rump with mash and salad. Craig says thank you. And asks Russell, if he'd like another beer? 'Ooh! Give me a second my dear.' Russell gives Craig a thumbs up, points to his phone, then points towards the exit. He stood up and moved out into the lobby.

- "Sorry about that interruption, please go on."
- "What was that about a beer? You two are not just carelessly drinking are you?"
- "No! We arrived just in time to sit down for dinner. We're being responsible. Now, 'Mr Thompson's Chair' is a story. You remember when Joanna[4] had trouble sleeping in the past? We always read either 'The Palace of Princes' or 'The Goblin Bridge.' And they settled her."

-   "Yeah."

"Well, that night during that storm. I reached for 'The Palace of Princes' like usual. Only it didn't work. "I found myself surrounded, suddenly it wasn't just Joanna, her brothers joined in. Now I was outnumbered too. "They asked for 'something new.'[sighed] "Similar thing to you, I too just wanted to get to bed. "My mind blank! I couldn't think of anything. [quieter] The rain seemed to have slowed down. Anyway, I began talking about how I was feeling, what I was thinking.

-   [yawns] "Which was?"..... Mummy!... "Give me a minute, Russell." Cherry, calls out, I'll be there soon. I'm just speaking with your father..... What? Ok, I'll tell him, quiet now. "Jo says. 'I love you daddy.' "Go on, your feelings/thoughts."
-   "Of how I'm the luckiest man in the world. Being married to their mummy. Surrounded by three adorable monsters."

I continued on to say. "Kids you won't find this story on any library shelf. Because it's the true story of 'Mr Thompson's Chair.' "Mr smarty, Bradley said. 'A chair! You sit in them, that's not a story! "I said let me finish. This story is so well known to me, in fact. "It's all about my favourite chair. "I created a story of how we met. "Picturing your face, seeing the cute faces of our children. "I guess my sub conscious narrated the story for me.

Cherry said, "I appreciate your sharing this with me. And you're ready to tell me the whole story. However I don't believe it would work. "I'm certain I couldn't tell it the same way you did. "I'll just go with a classic nursery rhyme. And promise them. That tomorrow night dad will tell us all the story of 'Mr Thompson's Chair' when he gets home. "Alright honey, you enjoy your dinner. Don't work too hard. [yawns] im gonna carry Frank [2]to bed."

- You know? Just one more thing. When I tell them our story. I always hear the same two questions.
- [Q1] Bradley asks "dad, Cheryl? Is that mum?"

I reply. "Yes Bradley, when I'd seen this fabulous person in my chair, my knees wobbled like jelly. [smiles] "It pleases me so, to be the one who pulls her chair out for her."

- [Q2] Joanna, "dad, you say 'curly auburn hair!' Was it pretty?"

I tell her. "Yes, sweetheart. It was a little bit longer than yours is now. But yours is curlier."

- "Thanks for sharing this with me dear. I'll see you tomorrow. I love you."
- "Love you too dear Cherry, goodnight."

Russell returned to the restaurant and re-joined Craig. "Sorry about that mate, there's a storm at home. "Cherry, was just asking what I do to comfort our kids?"

Chapter Twenty Seven

---⚜---

Winter Forth

Helen looked over at Jamie who is presently in his last year of high school. Jamie always loved manual arts, geography, and maths. Craig said he may become a travelling lawyer. His mum Helen disagreed. Suggesting he may become a conductor or an engineer. Due to this love/fascination with trains. At age 6 he built his first model railroad. Along our downstairs hallway. I've not travelled on many trains. But the way, one got under my foot. I tell you. I went for a ride! Jamie always enjoyed he's building blocks and Lego. But was always more intrigued by the numerous trains that regularly rocked on their way by to and from the station. For as long as Helen could remember. Jamie loved watching them pass. More so around 5pm, Wednesday's. That's when the express train travels pass. Jamie's already done his homework, gone for a short ride on 'Trifle' after leaving the stable. He sits on the front veranda and just watches the trains. From the veranda steps to their mail box is about 180-200m ish. The train tracks, trains can be clearly seen. Though on the opposite side of the road. The express trains are so shiny and elegant. He looks at the compartments, counts the carriages, and engines. Jamie has often found himself imagining about the lives of the travelling passengers. Then pondered these questions to himself:-

- Where they may be headed?
- Where'd they come from?
- Would they have a great love story to share?
- Or a tragic tale to tell?

Some passengers would wave out. Others just seemed to stare blankly out or their window. Most were reading a book, a newspaper or a magazine. Helen, gets home from work around 5pm. She is now manager of a small secretarial agency in Hillstem. Craig is already at home. lately he has been making minor renovations, odd re painting and remodelling the home office. He has also carried out some general maintenance on buildings down at 'Country Life'. Craig has been a carpenter for twelve plus years now. When looking out and around over the grounds of 'Winter Forth' as well as in their manor, some guest rooms of 'Country Life' bed and breakfast. You can see many items, Craig has personally handmade. In the garden by the BBQ area. There are outdoor benches, small tables. Those were created by Craig's father Logan. Much of the wood needed for Craig's project was sourced from the trees that grow along the back and or down the driveway. There's a furniture shop in Hillstem. 'Loungeabout' It has always been one of Craig's loyal customers. They stock love seats, coffee tables, dining chairs, study desks and kitchen cabinets. Craig has made some wooden bar stools and matching bedside tables. But not commercially. They stayed here, being placed at the bed and breakfast. Stools were around a communal outdoor table. For the past two weeks, Helen has been setting up a website. Partially to keep in touch with the contactors.

Craig had acquired whilst they were in Paris. Doing business with them, saw a spike in sales for 'Winter Timber Traders and sons' contractors and or new clients, customers could make orders and confirm supplies online. Craig arranged incoming and outgoing deliveries through a recently established local timber yard. Helen particularly enjoyed her personal tour through their onsite warehouse. She was amazed, a whole section contained full kitchens. Not just everything you could buy for a kitchen, im talking full display. Literally like walking into a working kitchen. Bench in the middle, top/bottom cupboards, double sink. An oven, microwave, toaster. A 6pce dining setting and chairs. The only things missing were the power and a door. And I'll bet they could have been arranged, if wished. Truly unbelievable, you could step into a bay. And announce "I'll take this one!" We're currently renovating and re furnishing 'Country Life' bed and breakfast. I would love to go wild in this place. If not for a kitchen... then to look at bedroom and bathrooms. Beside the items Craig or Logan made themselves. Much of the cosmetic decorations were done by myself, Lucy Renee and Meredith. Helen, can hear Craig calling her. Helen, looked around. Still hearing his voice but not seeing him. She followed the sound of his voice. Up onto the back veranda. Craig's voice asked "You like brown, burgundy or beige? Craig, was mentally hoping and wishing brown, brown, brown. "Brown", Helen replied. "Yes! Craig knew he'd be right about this. Helen found Craig in the kitchen. She knew he was working on something. But looking around, nothing seemed different. She turned around and went to leave. Craig asked, "so what do you think?" Helen[confused] "uh, it's nice, taller than I thought it would be..." she hoped he'd reply something, anything that may give her a clue. Statements like "tables are not meant to be tall!" Or "Now our coffee doesn't have to sit on the floor!" But no. Nothing. [puzzled] I said to Craig in my sexiest, mysterious voice. "Show me!" Craig walked over to the our microwave, bent down and opened the double cupboard doors underneath the bench. Ta da! "Oh! Honey, A new dishwasher, I love it. To the left there were four built in drawers. All brilliantly disguised behind chocolate brown facing boards.

Helen couldn't believe it. And [thought] that's what he's been up to. "All those questions; how big is our dishwasher? How long does it run for? Do you use the hose to fill it up, or tap? [sighs, shook her head] silly me. "I actually came to believe. He wished to know. So he could load and do the dishes for us while im at work. "I threw my arms around Craig. And said I love it, it's perfect. Thankyou my dear."

Chapter Twenty Eight

❦

Lucy and Louis's Wedding, 11th of June 2017

It seemed like only yesterday, Louis Sutton had whisked Lucy away for a weekend in NSW. Where Louis's family had thrown them a huge engagement party. When they'd returned home. Another grand get together awaited them. Organised by Lucy's parents Helen and Craig and their family. Now today Lucy and Louis are getting married at 'Winter Forth' unfortunately Minister Pierce has retired. His nephew, Beau will be performing the ceremony. Lucy's bestest friend, Suzie is her Maid of honour. The two brides maids are ladies she met at Tafe. Melissa and Claire. The dress that Lucy and her mother picked out is a pearly white colour. It features a v shape neck line and has gorgeous lace along the cleavage lines. And a yellow sash that ties in the back. Lucy designed the bouquets herself, all with fresh flowers and ferns from her garden. Her bride maids wore yellow as for Susan she wore a beautiful lilac dress. Each handmade bouquet has a single red rose in the centre, surrounded by a mix of white, yellow and light purple flowers. The men had a small lilac coloured rose on their grey suits with yellow Cummerbunds and ties. Louis's best friend Pete was his best man. His two groomsmen were; Lucy's brother Jamie. And Matthew a long-time mate of Louis's. Helen carried, Page boy Jacob Scott Sutton, [1 month, born 09/05/2017] Helen [thought] isn't this amazing? Im carrying page boy today. On my wedding day to Craig 08/05/1998. Flower girl Lucy was carried by [my sister] Aunty Mary. That evening at the reception. Craig stood up and made an announcement [clinking his glass] "friends, friends I wish you all to join me in congratulating the happy couple," (cheering) Craig raises his glass up, "to Mr and Mrs Sutton." [13th of June 2017], Whilst Louis and I are honeymooning in Fiji for three weeks. Mum [43] and dad [42] will be looking after our son Jacob. Logan [70] and Renee [66] still live in the cottage, that Mrs Sherwood had. They had the same feeling of excitement run through them. Like when mum and dad announced they were expecting me, A granddaughter. And they are over the moon at the idea of having Jacob, [their great grandson] around. To quote grandma Renee. 'it helps keep you young!'

- When I asked dad, "what was granddad Logan's reaction?"
- "honestly, I don't know how he took it. "He smiled, then walked out the front. Didn't say anything to me, didn't shout out a whoo hoo! "Granddad walked back inside 40 mins later. with the biggest grin on his face. "Still saying nothing, just made himself a cup of coffee. I sat next to him and asked. "Dad, where did you go? He [sipped his coffee] no reply. "I repeated. Dad, what happened?"
- "Nothing son [smiles] I was just looking out over the stables and my head begun to fill with visions of future pony shows, parades, riding lessons. "First day of school. Ah just to name a few."

Craig, hasn't heard much from his brother Wilson, since they moved to LA, USA, 6 months ago. His wife Monique, got hired as a personal shopper and fashion consultant for the ever glamorous……. Oh! [Silly me] "That's right, I'm not allowed to say! You'd think I would know better by now. "Aunty Monique, always said. 'Discretion, my dears. Discretion!' Come December the family will once again head off on Boxing Day for our annual 'Christmas camping trip.' Mum and dad are definitely going, joined of course by Jamie. Granddad Jerry, has expressed his desire to join only 'the fishing'. Then he'll return home. Me, Jacob and Louis gladly accepted our invitation. Monique, Wilson and their son Mark are unfortunately not able to come with us. But they did promise to be here for Christmas day and stay on, watching over 'Winter Forth' until mum and dad return. Having finished school, Jamie hasn't made any definitive plans. What we do know for sure is. The graduation present from mum and dad and his grandparents. [savings] was put towards a motor home. When mum asked

- "do you have any plans for settling down?"
- Jamie, [smiles] and jokingly replies, "not yet! I've still got half a tank of petrol…"
- [laughs] "There is plenty of room here at home. My boy. This farm does not run itself. You should remember what it requires."
- "Yeah stamina and strength. These come in handy for especially when your ordered to assist and not just on 'spring sapling Saturday' holidays. Jamie [laughs] thinking on the time his dad and uncle Wilson had to re plant the oak trees along the driveway."
- "Remember too, your granddad Logan and I were happy to help you build a small place of your own down the back."
- "I know dad. I'll think about it. But I do have my heart set on travelling."
- "I asked him why? "Where does this exploring bug come from? Don't you want to get a job?….. Date someone?"

Jamie looked at his watch. "Ooh! Almost 5pm. Over here dad. "Let's sit on the bench, near the turning circle. You watch with me. "The express train, soon will be rocking on by. [train approaches…

passing] Jamie continues, "See always moving, going somewhere. Different places, different people. You remember how I watched the trains faithfully when I was growing up?"

- "Yeah. I do."

"What I never told anyone was. That even then, I dreamt of travelling. "Just like they do. Well not exactly the way they do. "But in my motorhome 'Wandering Willow' is like an express train to me. It has an engine, a carriage and a passenger. "With many tales to share. Both ideas involve freedom, independence. "When people see me driving around. They may ponder the very same questions "I had as I watched passengers pass by on these trains."

- "I'm all for travel, exploring different places, seeing historical sights. "I also know 'it's wonderful having someone beside you for the journey.' "And a place you can go home to. And no! young, "Mr Winter. I'm talking of a real home. "Not just moving from the front seat to the rear seat and saying 'I'm home!'"

"Well, ... promise you won't say anything to mum yet. But I may...... bring someone with me for Christmas day. "I did ask her about bringing a friend? And she probably thought just that, 'friend!' I'm hoping this person is one day a little more than a friend." Later that afternoon Craig joined Helen in the kitchen. Craig made a coffee then took off to the garage. Lucy came in and sat with her mother at the kitchen table.

- "Mum, I don't know how factual it is. "But I just overheard Jamie telling dad that for Christmas day, he will have a +1."
- We looked at one another [cheekily giggled] then surprisingly at the same time said,

- "I wonder if its Agatha?"

For months now, unbeknownst to Jamie. When telling his stories. He's often added 'someone phrases' ever since 'Wandering Willow' [his motorhome] had some minor engine trouble. Helen took it as if Jamie was sharing more than he wanted with us all. Because just after saying it. He'd correct himself [like he made a mistake.] or just smile to himself. I personally have not heard of or used the term someone in such a pleasing manner. Jamie was ready to leave the Sandgate RV trailer park. But 'Wandering Willow' wouldn't start. The trailer park, is owned and operated by the Patterson family. Agatha, is their 19 year old daughter. She works in the reception, and does cleaning. At times Agatha has done personal shopping for residents. The most interesting tales, Helen recalls were.

- "I had to get 'someone' to drive me down to the mechanics." And "I needed to stay, until my part arrives. Me and 'someone' often took afternoon walks along the beach." But the one that got Jamie all lit up like when he was 5 and it's Christmas morning. "Was when he told us 'someone' absolutely adored the chicken stir fry I made for her. Ah for dinner I mean."

Helen [giggled]to herself, and said "I know no one is pleased with flood water. But last month, I couldn't get home for three days? I stayed with Jamie in Runegate. "The first day, Jamie [rubbed his hands together] and asked me 'what's for dinner, mum?' I think he saw an opportunity to enjoy a home cooked meal again. I told him, 'it'll be whatever you're making!' We headed to the local supermarket. Where I believe all meals begin. Some people plan meals differently. I get inspired speaking to the butcher, seeing fresh produce, mixing and making my own sauces. I asked, 'Jamie. What do you feel like?' Now, either he didn't understand my question or he believed us to be in some large take away restaurant. He replied. 'hamburger and chips.' I just [laughed], stood back and repeated my question. He repeated his desire. 'Jamie, they have all those here. Only it's not going to be bought to you.' 'Let's get beef patties, round buns, salad items and a frozen bag of chips.' When we got home, Jamie threw himself onto the lounge and turned on the TV.

-     'Whoa! Uh, uh. These need putting away.'
-     '[urgh]' Jamie got back up.

When he opened the fridge. I was surprised how bare it was. [2 hours later] I called out to Jamie! 'Dinner.' He looked around [as if thinking, where?] 'Come on boy, were gonna make, well you're gonna make dinner.' He needed encouragement, guidance but we enjoyed our burgers and fries. The next day, I asked him what he'd like for dinner? He asked for my keys, and said 'I'll show you!' turns out that boy of mine. Takes leaps, not small steps. He wanted a roast chicken. [present day] To this day, I'm so pleased that I couldn't leave. Those three days, us cooking together. We bonded, caught up like old best friends. Before we parted company. Jamie mentioned how one day Agatha wishes to have children. Born prematurely, her parents had difficulty falling pregnant again. However her mother and father have cared for and raised two foster children over the years. I attempted to bring up the subject of settling down again. I got his standard response. 'I know mum, I'm good!'

Chapter Twenty Nine

‡

6th of November 2018, Remembering Becky

Sitting out the front of the cottage at 'Winter Forth' Helen began thinking back on her mother uncontrollably. She saw, her running around the garden with Jamie and Lucy. The week she'd spent, supporting me. When I was pregnant with Jamie. Helen walked back inside, sat down in the lounge room and decide to give her Father jerry a call.

- "Hi dad, next week Craig and Wilson are going to Tempurst reserve, for a fishing trip. I thought you might like to join them?"
- "Nah, thanks anyway love. "Tell that husband of yours he can drop me off a fish though."[chuckles] (Silence..., papers rustling)
- "Dad?, dad! Are you still there...?
- "Just tidying up some old papers of your mother's."
- "I said me and Mary would come help you do that!"
- "I appreciate that. I was looking for something specific. Figured I may as well. "I have the box out anyway! more rustling, tossing, slight bang,] "What do we have here? A poem." [a long upset sigh]
- "Poem?"

"Your mum wrote many poems. Poetry was a love she and Jamie shared. "That one that he read at her funeral was just one. "It seemed those two had their own language. I often found Becky in her favourite chair, Jamie sitting beside her. "He quoted words aloud, she was writing them down. "The way they read through together. Looked like an actor, rehearsing his script. "I couldn't make them out. The only words I did understand were 'sorry, were we too loud?'

- "This poem that you found, is it one they created together?"
- [Reading, to himself]
- "No dear. This poem, mum wrote for me after our engagement. "Each anniversary she'd recite to me. "We believed it was lost. But.. "Helen, do you remember all those shoe boxes that sat at the base of her coats and dresses?"
- "Yeah, the ones that contain everything but shoes!"

"That's them! I began looking through them, one by one. "I was doing this when you called. Still not seeing the papers for our car. I reached for the very last box, toward the back. "No car paperwork! Jewellery, various small photos, a stack of, "I assume every comb she ever owned! Our poem was in amidst some postcards. When I unfolded it, a dried rose just about leapt out onto my lap. [chuckles] "I can't believe she kept, it all this time."

- "Please tell me about this special rose dad."
- "Like an exotic Spanish dancer, I had 'this rose' between my teeth as I proposed to her. "I was so nervous, I'd almost talked myself out of it. "We'd only been together six months and Trevor, her dad. "I don't know if you'd remember him. "Anyway, he gave me a hard time. "Something about running off with his only daughter."

- "It worked out. Mum accepted and dad, you and her had 34 years beautiful years together."
- "She did, this one night in April, I took her to one of her favourite restaurants. It felt right. I struggle to believe it at times. "That she actually said yes. [crying...., sniffs] I miss her so much Helen, she was well is the love of my life and my best friend."
- "I know, I miss her so much too. Mum always did know just what to say.... Even if it wasn't what they wanted to hear!"
- [laughs] "That she did Helen. I'll drop by to see you all soon before I go."
- "Go!"
- "Not this Sunday but the next I'm going to stay with your uncle Mason for a while."
- Alright dad, I'll see you then. Oh! Dad, one more thing. "Are you going to read me that poem? Or do I need to wait, until it's in one of your shoeboxes?"
- "Unnecessary, my dear. Besides, the only boxes I keep. Are usually on me.
- They both laugh..

Jerry begins to read.

First sight.
Darling, This love we have is a wonderful thing.
Can we start our celebrating?
At first I'll sing, then settle in your arms,
Where, I'll explore all your charms.
Though it's been a couple of months, plus sweet days,
I've fallen in love so many different ways.
No words can describe this feeling I have, when I'm with you,
But I'm already believing how much our love is true.

There may be distance between your age and mine
But we don't mind, for if our love were a crime,
Then, I'd plead guilty till the end of time.
But!
Hopefully we never meet the end, for you are my special
friend.

Jerry, [sniffling, sigh] continues.

But if the day comes,
I'll hold you in my arms, trying to stay strong, hoping
you can hold on.
We've been through so little, and it will never change
the way I feel.
I'm glad were together now, which shall,
Endure until my dying day.
My love for you will never stop! No way.

First sight, by Becky Cook, April 1965.

- Jerry [crying]. "Dad! Dad, are you ok?"
- [sniffs] "Yes, Helen. Don't get me wrong, I appreciate she's
  no longer in pain. There are times like… yesterday. "I cut
  the grass, looked toward the kitchen window. No smiling
  face happily waving back at me. Those memories are hard
  to face at times."
- "I understand, I've said to myself, 'we don't realize what
  we have until we don't have it anymore.' Gosh! "Hearing
  this out loud. Makes it sound like my mum was an old car
  or a piece of replaced furniture."
- "It's alright girl, I know what you meant. Love you."

Chapter Thirty

v

Homecoming. 8th of April 2019, Easter weekend

After getting his chores done, Craig sat quietly watching TV in the lounge room. Suddenly Helen rushes in and very excitedly announces "They're all able to come. They'll be here! [she, turned to dash away] Craig, says. "Wait, hold up. What?"

- "Easter weekend, Friday the 19th until Tuesday the 23rd of April. "They're able to be spend Easter with us."
- "Ah! Easter. "So that's what you and Monique have been doing! "Makes total sense now. As to why I couldn't get into our kitchen for near two days. "Fortunately, Jamie arrived when he did this arvo. Allowed me to make a coffee in 'Wandering Willow'. I assumed, you ladies were painting the kitchen."
- "Painting, yes! But just eggs, not the walls!"
- Craig laughed then said. "That's what transferred from your shirt to my overalls yesterday, food colouring! I'm also happy to announce that, Russell is bringing Gnome and Wilma with him."
- Helen, puzzled asked. Remind me Craig. "Who are Gnome and Wilma?

"Kenneth and William. I've spoken of them and their letters. "But you didn't actually meet them. "They were with Russell and me at Ashhern university. "Russell got a friend request from them through Face book. I look forward to catching up with them it's been so long." I spoke with Lucy this morning. Louis is on maternity leave with her. Big brother Jacob is a proud little helper. He tidies up, offers to carry things.

[laughs] do you remember when he stayed here last month?," Helen is now sitting beside Craig. "Jacob's toys were all up and down our hallway. Lately, he's put them away. Finally using the double toy chest Great grandpa Logan made him."

- "You know my darling. When I spoke to Lucy, Monday. She told me 'I can't wait for you to see Madeline' [Maddy]. Lucy expressed 'how she wished you were beside her in the hospital, born 05/02/19. Craig leans onto Helen's shoulder. Lastly, Lucy said 'Messengar, face book or snap chat are well enough for updates. But compared to face to face. It just isn't the same.'"
- "I agree with her Craig, smile, hug and laughter emoji's. I'll be crying real tears, smiling and hugging..."

18th April 2019 [Ding!, ding.] Craig checks his mobile. [reading aloud] it's from Louis. *"He's concerned Maddy may be fussy along the long ride. What shall we do dad?"*

Reply; *"As much as possible. Travel through the night, or just before dark. And she should sleep most of the way."*

- Thank you for that reply. I forgot, we had to do with Jamie. Huh? For someone set on travelling and adventure. He didn't like it then!"
- "You're welcome Craig dear. "But it's you whose usually helping everyone. Help Russell, assisted Marcus with the

horses. "You were the one who suggested your mum and dad [Logan and Renee to move into the cottage once Mrs Sherwood finally gave in to her sister Louise and moved in with her in 2017. The last time we had many people here was for Lucy's wedding."

- "Don't forget Helen. Many people, yes. Not all of them are staying. Well not staying here at least. We'll manage dear."

Craig, stood up from his chair. Had a full stretch, gave Helen an embracing hug [they kiss each other] Helen said, "your right! It will all be great. "I can hardly wait to see everyone. I love you. I love you too, my honey.[they cross their fingers] "Hopefully Jamie has some 'wonderful'... may regard a girlfriend. "Because when he first called to confirm. There was such excitement in his voice." Craig, began to head to the front yard. Helen grabbed his arm. And said. Hold on.

- "There is just one more thing, I'd like to discuss. Before people begin showing up."
- Craig, "Do you think, this is the holiday. We should finally reveal to our children, our photo"?
- "Our photo? You mean our portrait, that was done in Paris?"
- "Yeah, maybe it won't be as bad as we thought!"
- "Ok, I agree. Though I think it best you handle the reveal."
- "Just me! It's us, Mr winter. "Your just as guilty as I am, regarding what we did!"
- "It will be fine. Lucy will understand. And Jamie..... Ah?... Jamie?"
- "Exactly!, Jamie. I have no idea if I have the heart to tell our son. "That his parents were 'train bandits'.."

Craig, left the room and returns holding something in his hand. He stands beside Helen, holds up their portrait, shows it to her and says "correction, we were.....what?..."

- They say together "Sexy, glamorous train bandits."
- We certainly were! Agreed Craig. [They both laugh]

The end

ABOUT THE AUTHOR

Racheal Cardiss is a mother of four young adults. A carer and has aspirations of becoming self-employed in the future. As a party and event planner. Her interests are swimming, singing, toastmasters and painting. Rachel was born in NSW and moved to rural Queensland at 14. Where she resides today. It was whilst attending school there, her passion for writing begun. First short stories, then poetry. Racheal credits much of her determination, positivity, creativity. And some would say [stubbornness] to looking up to and revering her grandfather [deceased]. Racheal has completed a certificate 3 in community services and is also currently studying for a 'diploma in counselling'.

Rachel, has her own you tube channel and last year created a podcast. 'Carer's Caress' With the expressed desire to comfort, support and uplift fellow care givers. Who like herself provide care for a loved one- struggling with mental health. During times, Racheal was writing. If she'd got unnecessarily interrupted or disturbed. She replied "not now, I want to see what happens next!" [laughs]

Milton Keynes UK
Ingram Content Group UK Ltd.
UKHW020803231024
450026UK00001B/162

9 781963 883770